Transformed By Love

Transformed By Love

The Soul's Journey to God
in
Teresa of Avila
Mother Aloysius
of the Blessed Sacrament
Elizabeth of the Trinity

Shirley Darcus Sullivan

New City Press

For Mary
Mater Thesauri Cordis

Published in the United States by
New City Press, 202 Cardinal Rd., Hyde Park, NY 12538
www.newcitypress.com

Cover design by Nick Cianfarani

Library of Congress Cataloging-in-Publication Data:

Sullivan, Shirley Darcus, 1945-
    Transformed by love : the soul's journey to God in Teresa of Avila, Elizabeth of the
Trinity, and Mother Aloysius of the Blessed Sacrament / Shirley Muriel Sullivan.
       p. cm.
    Includes bibliographical references.
    ISBN 1-56548-168-2
    1. Mysticism--Catholic Church--History. 2. Carmelite Nuns--Biography. 3. Women
mystics--Biography. 4. Teresa, of Avila, Saint, 1515-1582. 5. Elizabeth of the Trinity,
Sister, 1880-1906. 6. Aloysius du Saint-Sacrement, máre. I. Title.

    BV5082.3.S85 2001
    248.2'2'0922--dc21   2001051217

Printed in Canada

Contents

Preface

This book offers a "strand of pearls," discovered by three women of Carmel. This "strand" by its beauty, intricate variety, and exquisite loveliness, teaches us much about the soul's journey to light. Jesus is the "light of the world" and we are all called to know and to love him. The "light" to which the soul journeys suffuses the universe with its divine presence. It also abides deep within each soul, acting as the source of its being, of its on-going transformation by grace, of the love it gives to others, and also as its ultimate goal.

The three women whom this book treats are Saint Teresa of Avila (1515–1582), Blessed Elizabeth of the Trinity (1880–1906), and Mother Aloysius of the Blessed Sacrament (1880–1961). These Carmelites found the "pearl of great price" that Jesus mentions (Matt. 13:45). For this "pearl," Jesus tells us, we go and sell all that we possess, so valuable and precious is it seen to be. These three Carmelites did not merely find the pearl but examined and cherished it. On seeing its true value, they sold all for it.

These women lived very different lives. Teresa was active in the sixteenth century. Blessed Elizabeth and Mother Aloysius were born in the same year of the nineteenth century, yet Elizabeth died very young, at twenty-six, while Mother Aloysius lived until she was eighty-one. All three women offer in their writings rich insights into the spiritual life. Again we see a great difference among them. Teresa is very well known. Elizabeth's writings have only recently become widely available. Mother Aloysius' sayings are not well known as yet. This book hopes to make the lovely strand of valuable pearls that these women found available to the reader. In learning of the spiritual truths they found, we will come, I hope, to understand, in a deeper way, the "soul's journey to light."

Introduction:
The Call of the Soul

Arise, my dove, my love,
my beautiful one
and come.

(*Song of Songs,* 2:10, 13)

In the sixteenth century a woman of vigor and energy reformed an existing religious order dedicated to Our Lady of Mount Carmel. Saint Teresa of Avila (1515–1582) was to make many foundations of her new order of men and women. Their call was principally to be people of prayer. To aid them in the endeavor she wrote several works, in particular *The Interior Castle*.

The Order of Carmel, over the centuries, was to produce three Doctors of the Church, Teresa herself, Saint John of the Cross, and Saint Thérèse of Lisieux. Many varied aspects of the life of prayer were treated by these saints. This order has produced other authors of works of great value for those interested in the spiritual life. Two of these are Blessed Elizabeth of the Trinity (1880–1906) and Mother Aloysius of the Blessed Sacrament (1880–1961).

This book will treat one main theme: how God dwells as light and love in each soul and how the soul, transformed by love, shares this love with others. First, it will describe what Teresa considered the soul to be like. Second, it will describe what Mother Aloysius says about God's careful training of this soul. Third, it will discuss Elizabeth's teaching on the response of the soul to God's loving presence within it and the ways in which the soul shares love with others.

By its examination of wisdom from Carmel, this study hopes to help those desiring to grow spiritually. In these three writers we encounter experts in the life of holiness. Their insights and vision can help us as we journey toward heaven, the goal of each of us. Everyone is at a different stage of growth with regard to the spiritual life. What these Carmelites say may help us now or in the future. In their works we can find answers to many questions about the spiritual journey. Both in sum and in part they can light our path.

The Carmelites chosen for study, whether very well known like Teresa, generally well known like Elizabeth, or little known like Mother Aloysius, give us "pearls of great price" (Matt. 13:45)[1] as we hope to show.

Background: The Soul

Our focus in this book will be upon the soul. First, we can say that what we find in these Carmelite authors is a traditional, Christian view of the soul. They all have been much influenced by earlier teachings about the soul and make certain assumptions in the light of these teachings.

As is widely recognized, the early Church Fathers and later Christian authors were profoundly influenced by Greek philosophy, especially Platonism and Neo-Platonism. In the development of Christian thought, therefore, we can discern both Jewish and Greek influences. In this regard, from an historical perspective, we can perhaps discern God's plan. The Jews in their writings (the Old Testament) were chosen to learn of the one God who related in a personal way to his people. They were called to share this knowledge with the nations. Among the gentiles the Greeks were to discover profound truths about the nature of divinity and the soul. The early Church Fathers, well versed in Greek thought, wisely adopted and adapted many insights of the Greeks into their own theological thinking. These insights were always in accord with the teachings found in the Old Testament but often added rich detail and perspective that enhanced those teachings.

One view in particular that they adopted was the Platonic view of the soul (*psyche*). By the time of Plato the term *psyche* had come to designate the seat of thought, emotion, and will within the person.[2] It was seen as the center of personality. Most importantly, this soul was considered to be a definite reality within the person. The soul within was, in a way, the "real" person. It was responsible for all conscious psychological activity. It alone survived after death in either a positive or negative state.

Only gradually had the Greeks come to such a notion of *psyche* both in the living person and after death. To see how the term *psyche* changed in meaning over the centuries is a fascinating study.[3] In early Greek literature *psyche* is simply the breath that keeps people alive. But it is also the only part of the person that survives after death. It does so as a pale shade or image of the person, floating around Hades, under the earth. Very early, therefore, *psyche* is associated with the survival of the person after death. Gradually *psyche* in the living person comes to have some psychological functions. It starts to act as a seat of thought and feeling. As time passes, *psyche* is still the part of the person that survives after death but it functions more and more prominently in people when they are alive. It starts to be the seat of thinking, feeling, and willing. For Plato the *psyche* within is the most precious possession of human beings. Their role is to recognize the crucial function of their *psyche* and to realize that *psyche* is their identity in this life. The nature of this *psyche* at death will determine their future destiny.

It is the Platonic view of *psyche*, as the seat of personality that becomes prominent in early Christian thought. It continues to be the view of the soul found in our Carmelite writers. In them, we hear much of the nature of the soul, its destiny, and its progress toward holiness. Plato speaks frequently of *psyche,* describing it in detail. As in Plato, the soul in our Carmelite authors is something real, the most important part of a person. It is this soul that is called to immortal life. The body will rise eventually but the soul will encounter God upon death. Christ thirsts for all souls, longing for their redemption. "Soul" signifies the whole person: thoughts, feelings, and movements of will. This soul during life is far from perfect. Time, as it passes, and all the circumstances of a life contribute in many ways to the transformation of the soul and its state at the time of death. It is this soul, in need of growth and change, that is the focus of attention of these three Carmelite women.

On the one hand, therefore, these Carmelites adopt a traditional and commonly accepted view of the soul. On the other hand, they offer many new ideas about its nature and function within the person. In each author we find various aspects of the soul described and clarified.

This book will treat these various Carmelite teachings about the soul. Teresa presents a detailed description of the nature of the soul, comparing it to an exquisite diamond, intricately structured. Mother Aloysius describes how this soul is made beautiful and holy by God's will of every moment. Elizabeth teaches how this soul is called on to surrender to the purifying action of God within, God who is love.

The Challenge of Love

These three Carmelites have much to say to Christians about our pilgrimage to God. Our souls are called to journey to the light. We are to encounter love, be suffused with divine love and to radiate it to others. These three Carmelites will teach us in particular how to love and how to be loved. Both of these are essential if we are to grow spiritually. To love is often difficult. To be loved is also challenging. Before studying what the Carmelites have to say, let us look at this question of loving: how are we to love and be loved?

Love is at the core of the Christian message and is the challenge of every person to express. The Christian message is clear: we are to love God, love our neighbor, and to love ourselves (Matt. 22:37–39). But the outward expression of love is only possible when people firmly believe that they are loved and are lovable. Yet people doubt both that they are loved and that they are lovable. As we look at human society, we see why this can be so. Often other people fail to love us. They do not even like us! If there are many treating us in this way, we can certainly begin to question whether we are lovable.

But what of God? How can we ever doubt that we are loved by God? We know that the Father sent his only Son to die for our sins. For each one of us Jesus suffered a cruel and painful death on the cross. Surely God loves us! We must, therefore, in essence be lovable. That we are lovable is a core truth that greatly affects human motivation. Already in the second century we hear Saint Hippolytus assert: "One who is loved generates love."[4] It may not be too extreme to assert that *only* if we accept that we are lovable can we love others.

Sources of Doubts about God's Love

Why then do we doubt that we are lovable? This doubt, we can suggest, began with the Fall (Gen. 3:1–24). In the story of Adam and Eve we learn that there is something inherent in human nature that can say "no" to God. Drawn by what pleased the eyes and seemed attractive to the mind, human beings used their free will and made a choice. It was a wrong choice as consequences were to show. We gained a form of knowledge but the range of that knowledge proved to have devastating effects.

Human beings were now acquainted with both good and evil. They were now aware that they were capable of evil. Free will, most precious of gifts, became clear in its range. On the one hand, we can listen to God and obey. On the other hand, we can disregard God's voice and choose what may be contrary to the divine will and our own ultimate good.

If we choose the second course of action, are we still lovable? In the story of Adam and Eve God cares for them as they leave Eden, providing them with clothes (Gen. 3:22). But can we not imagine that these two people would wonder if they were still loved as they were loved before? The Fall left in the human heart a wound that would persist and prove very hard to heal. We can doubt that we are lovable, especially if we have done wrong and been disobedient to God's will.

If we gaze at human history as recorded in the Old Testament, we can detect an over-riding, general pattern. Human beings constantly strove to be good but constantly also did wrong. Again and again God calls human beings to observe the Law, a way of life that focused on goodness. But human frailty and distorted passions proved to be most persistent. On many occasions they failed to observe the Law. This Law, if followed, allowed human beings to behave well and to enjoy the happiness of peace with God. Its orders and prohibitions provided a protective context. They kept human beings from performing actions that would be wrong and would bring conflict and unhappiness. They guided human beings on paths that would lead to holiness and goodness.

If we glance in First Samuel at David, God's chosen, anointed one (16:13), we see the range of human choice of good and evil. David could soothe Saul with his music (16:23), perhaps singing what would become some of the Psalms. David had the courage to slay Goliath (17:1–51). He later braves the enmity of Saul and proves his steadfast loyalty (24:2–21). In Second Samuel we learn that David became a great king in Israel (5–24). But it is David who arranges the murder of Uriah in order that he could conceal his adultery with Bathsheba (11:2–26). Later David repents of his actions and does penance (12:13–23). In this whole situation God's faithfulness remains sure. The promises made to David and his house (7:1–17) abide despite his wrong-doing. God says: "I will not take my steadfast love from him" (7:15). David, most beloved of God, proves capable of great evil. God's love does not change. David's thankfulness on being forgiven is far greater than any that he felt before. That God could and would love him "still," won his heart forever. He remained the "beloved." He rejoiced to find himself still lovable.

As we live out our personal destinies, we discover that we are like Adam, Eve, and David. We find within a great range for good

but also one for evil. Throughout the ages human beings tried
and tried to become holy by careful observance of the Law. But
such observance did not lead to the holiness that human beings
desired. Always the range for evil would prove present. Many
times a day human beings would fall.

Christ's Gift of Grace

With the coming of Jesus and by his sacrifice on the cross, the
grace of salvation entered the human experience. Human beings
found salvation from all their wrongdoing: we "are now justified
by grace as a gift" (Rom. 3:24). Human beings are not simply
saved from their sins but undergo a transformation into the
image of Christ (2 Cor. 3:18). We come to have the "mind of
Christ" (1 Cor. 2:16). We always retain the capacity to sin but, if
we do, we place confidence in the intercession that Jesus ever
makes for us (Rom. 8:34).

The Law has been replaced by the dispensation of grace. As
before, we human beings remain inwardly the same, capable of
good and evil. But now our situation is radically altered. We no
longer strive for perfection by observance of a Law, but move
slowly toward holiness by constant surrender to Christ's spirit,
the Holy Spirit, living in our hearts (1 John 4:13–16).

Old ways, however, are hard to change. So often, because we
are capable of evil, we have to strive mightily against the
tendency to do wrong. We prove capable of a form of self-hatred
that often yields negative results. Forgetting the lessons of grace,
we strive to overcome the negative aspects of self by following set
codes of behavior, rather in the manner of an observance of the
Law. Throughout the centuries of Christian history extreme
forms of asceticism have emerged and, on some occasions, have
been accounted virtue. Set codes of rules and regulations have
been formulated that seem to lead to growth in holiness. But
again and again we discover that these fail. It is not in the power
of human beings to make ourselves good. However much we
strive to control ourselves, check our emotions, and repress our

desires, self seems ever present and ever ready to reveal negative traits. We can come, perhaps, to have a totally hostile attitude to our inner self. We may even "hate" it. But this attitude can be harmful. How can we think ourselves lovable if we hate ourselves?

Jesus well recognizes that there are elements within the human person that are not admirable. We hear him tell us "to deny self" (Matt. 16:24). We even hear him say that we cannot be his disciples unless we "hate" our soul (*psyche*) itself (Luke 14:26).[5] But in these references Jesus does not teach that the core of the person is not good or lovable. In fact, in total contradiction to such a notion, he teaches us to love our neighbor in the same way in which we love ourselves (Matt. 22:37–39). If, however, we strive for holiness by attempting to mold our souls within by restraint and self-control, we may well come to believe that part of ourselves at least is not lovable. Is this true of a part of ourselves?

The Essence of the Human Being

When we discern in ourselves the capacity to be angry, to lie, to be deceptive or dishonest, to steal, or even to act violently, we must admit that such capacities are in no way lovable. How then are we to view ourselves as deserving the love of God and of other people? Here also Greek philosophy can be of help. As we mentioned above, the traditional Christian view of the soul traces its origins from Greek philosophy, especially that of Plato. In certain dialogues and especially in the *Protagoras*,[6] Plato describes Socrates as arguing for a particular view of human beings: at every moment that we act, we choose a "good." Even though individuals at times clearly perform actions that are evil, Socrates believes that at the specific time they act they are convinced that their action is the best for themselves. People may need to be taught or made to understand that their actions are not good either for themselves or others. If they learn that this is the case, their future actions would, he was convinced, be different. Education, therefore, is more needed for those who do wrong than any form of punishment.

Another view of Plato can prove helpful in confirming our conviction that we are lovable. In the *Symposium* Plato describes different kinds of love.[7] He introduces various forms and levels of love, ending the dialogue with a description of that which is noblest. This is the love that each soul has for beauty and goodness. In Greek the word for love, *eros*, actually means "a desire for" or a "longing for." Plato suggests that the essential core of each soul is a "longing for" beauty and goodness. We thus see two Platonic features of the soul of a person. First, at each moment human beings always choose a "good" of some kind and, second, all human beings "long for" beauty and goodness. The highest good that a person can choose is one related to the true beauty and goodness that are the source of or pattern for all existing things. The philosopher longs for this beauty and goodness in the same way that the Christian longs for God.

Whether these views of human beings are correct or not, they provide us with a helpful perspective in viewing the soul. What makes these views so attractive is their optimism. God, we may believe, has created human beings who are in essence, like the rest of his creation, "good" (Gen. 1:10, 12, 18, 21, 25). This seems particularly so since we are made in God's image (Gen. 1:27). Despite the Fall and its consequences, we can still be convinced that our souls are essentially "good" and our will is directed toward the Good. As such, we are essentially beautiful. We can understand why God always loves us. We can be convinced that in essence we are lovable. True, our wills can go astray. We have, therefore, a constant need to grow in knowledge and understanding so that we can choose the Good. Knowledge and understanding, just like counsel and wisdom, are gifts of the Holy Spirit. If we persevere in grace, these gifts will be poured into our souls. Time and again we may have to learn to forgive others for the wrong they do to us. So too we will need to learn to forgive ourselves for the evil or wrong that we do. And this, perhaps, is hardest. If, however, we are convinced that we are essentially "good" in soul, we will find the resources needed to pardon ourselves. Only if we forgive ourselves can we move forward in a positive way, convinced that we can be loved by God and others.

Growth in Holiness

In our spiritual journey, therefore, it is first essential to believe that we are lovable. Second, we have to recognize that abundant inner transformation must precede any state of holiness we may achieve. Growth in holiness for the Christian is a growth in grace. We learn to surrender more and more to the action of the Holy Spirit, making us like Jesus. For those seriously committed to the spiritual life, growth will occur. God "chastises and corrects those whom he loves" (Ps. 94:10; Heb. 12:6). Jesus says: "I reprove and discipline those whom I love" (Rev. 3:19). Paul describes himself as "being crucified with Christ" so that the "life of Christ" may be manifest in him (Gal. 2:19). And perhaps here is a key to understanding Christian growth.

Crucifixion in many forms will befall us during our lives. Sickness, failure, loss of loved ones, poverty, death: in a word, suffering in all its manifestations, is the lot of human beings. We are called to endure suffering and, optimally, to grow in it and from it. In the context of life, its joys and sorrows, happiness and pain, our focus needs to be one of surrender to love at work in our lives. Somehow, through all circumstances, we must hold firm one conviction: God loves us and we are lovable.

Yet, there will always be parts of ourselves that we know need to be changed. Our focus, however, is not to be on perfecting the acceptable parts of ourselves and crushing the unacceptable. Instead, Jesus calls on us to "deny" those unacceptable elements in us and not to allow them to flourish or thrive. Gradually, as Jesus grows within us by the working of the Holy Spirit, we are to forget our "self" altogether. Every moment, to the degree that we can, we are to focus on Jesus within and to follow the impulses of his will.

Love for Others

In our relations with others Jesus emphasized forgiveness. It is very easy to be aware of the negative traits in others and, equally, of their admirable features. The same range of good and evil in ourselves is evident in others. Jesus tells us both to love ourselves and to love others in the same way in which we love ourselves. Often, however, instead of loving one another, we hurt and harm one another. In such situations Jesus teaches us to pray to be forgiven in exactly the measure that we forgive. We are to overlook, therefore, the negative in others. Thus, too, it will be overlooked in ourselves. With forgiveness we can hold onto a truth about ourselves and about others: despite particular actions, we remain lovable. As we become convinced of this trait in ourselves, we look for it in other people. We begin to see with God's eyes.

If we accept that we are intrinsically lovable, we find resources within to love others. For the Christian there must be a strong desire to love. This desire must go beyond merely coping with those who dislike or hurt us. The will must be intensely focused within on the spirit of love. Only one response becomes possible in every situation. Let Jesus act. Let the Spirit act. Let all be love. We are loved infinitely by God and we, in turn, love. In this state we have come to do what Paul tells us: "Pray always" (Luke 18:1). This state indicates an advanced degree of spiritual growth but one to which we are all called. The choice is ours. Jesus says: "Listen! I am standing at the door, knocking: if you hear my voice and open the door, I will come in to you and eat with you, and you with me" (Rev. 3:20).

For spiritual growth we have seen that there are three essentials: love of God, love of neighbor, love of self. The last is especially important because it can so easily be incorrectly perceived. Love of self must be authentic. We must truly be convinced that our soul in its essence is lovable. We are not to imagine God or neighbor loving us because they do so generously despite our being basically unlovable. To some extent there may be in God's love or in neighbor's love a degree of overlooking of faults or failings. But God is passionately fond of us because we are lovable. "Arise, my dove, my love, my beautiful one and come" (Song of Songs 2:10, 13). This call is for every soul. It allows us to rush eagerly to God and to be determined to discern the beautiful in others. "You have ravished my heart" (Song of Songs 4:9). If we hold firmly to this truth of how God looks upon us, the incentive to grow in love becomes very strong.

The three Carmelite writers whom we are to discuss tell us much about the Christian journey as presented briefly above. Teresa describes for us the nature of the soul and how our will can move within the vast dimensions of it to discover God present within. Mother Aloysius gives us details on how this soul is purified by God's loving action of each moment. Elizabeth helps us to understand how to forget ourselves, to surrender to God's abundant love for us, to dwell with the Trinity in our souls, and to let love pour out to others. All three emphasize the importance of our relations with our neighbors: always, at all times to love. These Carmelites help us to grow in our love and knowledge of God. Like the water at Cana, we are to be changed to a rich wine that will enrich the lives of the people we meet.

Notes

1. All Bible references, unless otherwise noted, are taken from the *New Revised Standard Version* (Oxford and New York: Oxford Univ. Press, 1989).

2. On the picture of the soul in Plato, see in particular T. M. Robinson, *Plato's Psychology* (Toronto: Univ. of Toronto Press, 1970) and W. K. C. Guthrie, *A History of Greek Philosophy* (Cambridge: Cambridge Univ. Press, 1975), Vol. 4, esp. 434–561.

3. On the early Greek view of the soul, see my study, *Psychological and Ethical Ideas, What Early Greeks Say* (Leiden: E. J. Brill, 1995).

4. Saint Hippolytus, *Discourse on the Holy Theophany*, Office of Readings, January 8 in *The Liturgy of the Hours* (New York: Catholic Book Publishing, 1976).

5. Usually *psyche* in Luke 14:26 is translated as "life" but it could also refer to the "soul," the "inner self" of the person.

6. See the following recent translations of the *Protagoras*: B. A. F. Hubbard (London: Duckworth, 1982), 2nd ed., S. Lombardo and K. Bell (Indianapolis: Hackett, 1992) and C. C. W. Taylor (New York: Oxford Univ. Press, 1996).

7. Of the *Symposium* see the following recent translations: J. Benardete (Chicago: Univ. of Chicago Press, 2001), A. Nehemas and P. Woodruff (Indianapolis: Hackett, 1988), C. J. Rowe (Warminster: Ares and Phillips, 1998), A. Sharon (Newburyport, MA: R. Pullins Co., 1998), R. Waterfield (Oxford: Oxford Univ. Press, 1994).

1
Teresa of Avila:
Overview of the Soul

*Our soul is like a castle
made entirely out of a diamond
or of a very clear crystal.*

(*Interior Castle*, I.1)

In the introduction we suggested that the conviction that our souls are lovable is essential for spiritual growth. We have to believe that there is something within us that is intrinsically and basically beautiful. It is this that "ravishes" the heart of God. It is this in each of us that is part of God's overwhelming love for the world, a love so great that the Father sent his Son for our redemption (John 3:16).

Teresa of Avila wrote her book called the *Interior Castle* during a period of six months in 1577. It is perhaps her masterpiece in its description of mystical prayer. In it, in particular, we find a picture of the soul in all its exquisite beauty. What she says of the soul with its intricate structure is true for every human being. All of us are graced with such a soul.

Ah, the soul! So beautiful! So wonderful! Each made in the image of God: "In the image of God he created them, male and female he created them" (Gen. 1:27). As we described in the introduction, Teresa considers the soul to be the center of our identity. In it are located our thoughts, feelings, and will. Our soul within infuses us with life. To this soul Jesus brought salvation by his death on the cross. This soul survives death and may come to gaze upon God in paradise. It journeys to the divine light.

The Nature of the Soul

How does Teresa describe this soul? It is "like a castle made entirely out of a diamond or of a very clear crystal, in which there are many rooms" (283). Let us consider this image of the soul. First, it resembles a castle. Teresa, living in medieval Spain, has clearly been influenced by her age and setting. She sees the soul as a magnificent structure, fortified, complex, strong. The soul, thus, in a way is a fitting dwelling place for God. Second, the castle is made of "crystal or diamond." The beauty of these two substances depends upon light. Crystals and diamonds have many facets and the greater their number, the greater the beauty of the stones. Look at a diamond. Hold it up to the light. See how it sparkles, the light catching its many surfaces. Turn the diamond slowly, marveling at its variegated beauty, each facet refracting the light in a different way. The complex structure of the diamond continues within. The inside of the diamond remains a mystery but its nature contributes to the refraction of light of the whole diamond.

Only in the light does a diamond display its wondrous nature. Put it in some dark place and its remains simply a dark stone. This is the first feature of the diamond that teaches us something about the soul. To see the beauty of the diamond, a source of light is essential. The more intense the light, the more the beauty of the diamond is revealed. Without light we do not know that the diamond is even a diamond nor do we detect its essential nature.

In the case of the soul the light that illumines it is of divine origin. Light streams from God revealing the complicated, multi-faceted nature of the soul. One image of this light, found mostly in Mansions 1–3 of the *Interior Castle*, is that of a light in the center of the soul radiating out to fill the whole structure. It shines most intensely at the center but can extend all the way to the furthest extremities of the soul.

A second image, associated especially with Mansions 4–7 of Teresa's work, is that the diamond itself is ever held inside a source of light like a small speck caught in a bright aura. Just as God cares deeply for his creation (Sir. 16:22–18:6) and his universe is tenderly held in his infinite embrace, so every soul actually exists in such a setting. We are each a jewel located in a fine setting, namely in God's very nature. "In him we live and move and have our being" (Acts 17:28). Thus we can be described as a "signet ring" that God cherishes (Hagg. 2:33). We are the stone in a rich and fine setting.

The diamond of the soul exists ever within this source of inner light but the nature of some of its parts may prevent the light from penetrating. These parts prove unreceptive to the light. For Teresa the light is God. In one way God or light is at the core of the diamond. As such, God is the goal of a person's spiritual journey on earth. In another way God or light is the immense setting of the soul which the soul will come gradually to know. As Teresa says:

> And in the center and the middle is the main dwelling place where the very secret exchange between God and the soul takes place. (284)

> Turn your eyes toward the center, which is the room or royal chamber where the King stays. (291)

It is easy to keep our eyes only on ourselves and to see ourselves as distinct entities. We may look too at the universe as made up of separate and discreet parts. But, correctly seen, all exist in the divine, enlivened and suffused by God.

The diamond teaches us more about the soul. It has multiple facets. Its structure is most complicated. Teresa compares this inner structure of a diamond to the description of heaven as having "many mansions" (John 14:2). The soul, then, as a crystal or diamond has many rooms within. This parallel that Teresa suggests can be analyzed on two levels. First, the soul itself has many parts or "rooms." Our inner structure is complicated, built in a diverse way. The rooms do not lie in a row, but like facets in a diamond, "some are up above, others down below, others to the sides" (284). Second, Teresa envisions, it seems, our moving through these rooms, ideally heading toward the center. She speaks of people being in the "outer courtyard" (285), not going inside, or even being aware of, the castle. They do not "enter within themselves at all" (286). For the inward journey she refers, as parallels, to descriptions that call on the soul "to enter within itself" (286).

Can we understand more explicitly what this entry into the soul involves? An understanding of this point helps us to grasp more exactly Teresa's picture of the soul.

The Inward Journey

Once again a glance at earlier traditions of thought can prove helpful. Early in Greek philosophy the notion appears of the human soul changing from an impure to a pure state. In the *Republic* Plato describes different kinds of souls—iron, bronze, silver and gold—and suggests that ideally all souls will become gold. Souls that have become gold are capable of gazing upon absolute goodness and beauty. Somehow our earthly life functions as the means by which the soul alters, slowly becoming more pure and beautiful.

In the Christian view the soul, saved by Christ's passion and death, grows in holiness during its earthly existence. Basically we can speak of the journey of the soul to God. This journey may be long, its path tortuous and difficult but the goal is clear. At death, depending on the state of the soul at that time, purgatory and further purification await, or paradise with the beatific vision of God.

Long before Teresa Christian writers had studied this journey of the soul. These writers include: Gregory of Nyssa (c. 330–c. 395), Evagrius of Pontus (346–399), Pseudo-Dionysius the Areopagite (fl. c. 500), Maximus the Confessor (580–662),

Bernard of Clairvaux (1090–1153), Hugh of St. Victor (1096–1141), Bonaventure (c. 1217–1274), Meister Eckhart (c. 1260–1328), John Ruysbroeck (1293–1381), Richard Rolle (1300–1349), and Walter Hilton (1340–1396). What becomes clear in the works of these authors is that the journey of the soul to God involves also a journey of the person within this soul.

But what is it that makes the journey? Both in earlier authors and in Teresa herself the answer appears to be the "will." By conscious choice and focused attention we can, it appears, journey through the mansions of our soul. In the first mansion the actions of our will prove to be highly important. In the more inward mansions God's action upon our wills proves to be crucial. At any time, by our will and choices, we can fall "back" and abide again in the first mansions, even though we had moved beyond them. In contrast, drawn by God we can go into the other, more distant, mansions. Our wills are a crucial part of the journey and are themselves slowly transformed by the journey. Gradually our will and God's will become identical. Our wills, however, remain ever distinct from God. We never become God. We remain creatures, free by nature, but we become ever more holy and beautiful.

Activity of the Will

Let us glance more closely at the activity of the will within the structure of the soul. Once again Plato's ideas prove helpful. In the *Republic* (Bk. 7, 514a–521b) we find the image of the cave used by Plato to describe the condition of different human beings. The source of light within the cave is a fire burning in its center. The source of light outside the cave is the sun. Some people are deep within the cave capable only of gazing at shadows cast on a wall by artefacts behind them and outside their range of vision. These people never encounter real objects at all. In fact they are twice removed from such real objects. They see only images of artefacts that themselves are modeled on real things.

A second group of people, still within the cave, can look at these artefacts themselves. These people too do not gaze on real objects but only on those patterned after them. Thus too, like the first group, they do not encounter reality itself. Yet a third group are found at the entrance of the cave, looking on objects in our world which are made visible by the sun. Those in this group are seeing real objects, no longer gazing simply at images or patterns. The fourth group, few in number, are able to step outside the cave and gaze upon the sun itself. The sun is the ultimate reality. It makes all objects visible and instills life by its heat and light.

Although Plato refers to the condition of different groups of people, this image of the cave could apply to the journey of a single individual. Taking the image of the cave—its inner structure, entrance and environs—as a picture of the soul, we encounter a person able to have different experiences on a spiritual level. Someone can direct all attention to "shadows on a wall" that partake in reality only in limited way. How quickly we might think of how much time people in our society spend watching television! With such a focus individuals may turn no attention to spiritual subjects. Others may turn from mere images and study the artefacts within the cave. Again these objects partake only partially in reality. These objects are more real than shadows on a wall but still are only patterns of reality. We can compare this group to those who attend only to worldly objects and events with no thought of their cause or meaning.

At a third level people may look at real objects in the world. In spiritual terms these are people who recognize spiritual realities. These are made visible by real light, that is, by the sun itself. These spiritual realities, once studied, make clear the limited nature of objects at the first and second levels. Such objects partake to some degree in reality but appear simply as images or patterns of what is truly real.

At the highest level people may gaze on the sun, the source of light itself. These people, in spiritual terms, have come to see God. In the cave itself all light in fact stems from this sun. Human beings are by nature drawn to this light of the sun but not all move toward it. Some are satisfied with only a glimpse of reality. Others are led to want more. A few strive to see the whole picture.

In Plato's image of the cave, people can choose the focus of their attention. He suggests that those who have moved out of the cave to gaze upon the sun have made a meaningful journey. These people are philosophers, "lovers of wisdom." They "see the sun." They have beheld the source of beauty and truth, the "Good" itself.

This picture of movement within and without the cave parallels what Teresa says of movement within the soul. She suggests that people can stay "outside the castle" (285). Others move into the palace of the soul and journey to the center "where the King stays" (291). The body, she calls, the "outer wall of the castle" or the "diamond's setting" (284). The soul, found within this body, is the location of the movement of the will. Each person at each moment is somewhere, either "outside" the castle or within.

What is totally original in Teresa is her detailed description of this journey within the soul. No one before had traced with such careful precision how the "will" could move through the various parts of the soul. With her image of the castle she suggests the complexity of the soul. With the idea of the journey within it, she tells how a person can grow spiritually and have deep experiences of God.

Another feature that is original with Teresa is her description of the "mansions" of the soul. Each mansion can be interpreted as the identity of a person at any moment of their lives. Jesus says: "Where your treasure is, there is your heart also" (Matt. 6:21). According to Teresa the "will" can be outside of the castle or it can move within it. At first, as we will see, it strongly chooses where it is to be. Later, if it persists in its spiritual journey, it will be strongly drawn inward by God's action. But it ever remains free. It may move "out" or "in." It may decide to give up the spiritual quest altogether. Or, it may, with all energy and vigor, strive for higher things. Whatever its choice, it determines what a person is at every moment. We are all somewhere on a spiritual quest. Even those who disclaim that this is so in fact are spiritually where their will happens to be in relation to the castle of the soul.

In Teresa's view, who we are at each moment is where we are either outside or inside the mansions of the soul. As was mentioned in the introduction, Socrates suggests that whoever we are and wherever we are, we are choosing what we consider to be a "good." In a way Teresa suggests the same. People whose wills are outside the castle are there because of what they choose. These individuals set a high value on worldly power or possessions. These are in their eyes "good." So, as people move through the various mansions to God at the center, they choose or are drawn to what they consider "good" at each stage. The awareness that who we are is exemplified by what we choose proves most helpful for spiritual growth. Teresa suggests a process of growing more and more aware of what is truly valuable. We move from attachment to lesser "goods" to the highest good, God. Plato, as we say, suggested in the cave image in the *Republic* that the person should turn from mere reflected light to the brightest of realities, light itself or the "Good." Teresa also envisions such a journey of persons within themselves. They too are in search of the light, the presence of God within.

Growth in Love

In the *Interior Castle* Teresa describes a journey through mansions to an encounter with God at the center of the soul. Above we suggested that it is the "will" that makes this journey. What happens to the will? Gradually it comes to be identified with the divine will. This will is love. "God is love and those who abide in love abide in God, and God abides in them" (1 John 4:16). What is to be the object of the will's love? Moses tells us to love the Lord our God "with all our heart, soul, and might" (Deut. 6:14). Jesus says the same: "Love the Lord your God with all your heart, soul, and mind" (Matt. 22:37). He adds also: "Love your neighbor as yourself" (Matt. 22:39). Elsewhere too Jesus adds a new commandment: "Just as I have loved you, you also should love one another" (John 13:34).

In Deuteronomy chapter 30, verses 1 through 20, Moses speaks of the effects upon the people of totally loving God. "The Lord your God will circumcise your heart and the heart of your descendants, so that you will love the Lord your God with all your heart and with all your soul, in order that you may live" (16). "Choose life so that you and your descendants may live, loving the Lord your God, obeying him, and holding fast to him; for that means life to you" (20). He also says that the "commandments and decrees" (10) they are to observe are in their very being: "The word is very near to you; it is in your mouth and in your heart for you to observe" (14).

This passage mentions two features of the will which likewise form a part of Teresa's description of its journey through the mansions. First, and most importantly, the will is free to choose. Moses urges people to choose to love God. They can turn their hearts elsewhere but the best course is to love God. Second, the will is gradually transformed by its very choices. Moses identifies the choice of loving God with a choice of "life." He says that when people "love God with all their heart and soul," they will "live."

Teresa describes the will as travelling through many mansions to a center where God is found. In the first three mansions we hear much of its choice of virtuous activity and of prayer. In the fourth to seventh mansions the will learns more and more to surrender to the action of God. The will still chooses to practice virtue and self-control. But it yields in ever greater degree to the purification that God effects. Slowly the individual and divine will become identified, although they remain distinct. The will in the seventh mansion is filled with God's love and itself loves God and neighbor as perfectly as is possible. It has been transformed into the "image of Christ" (2 Cor. 3:18), ready to serve the Church.

How can the human being encounter God at the center of the soul? More and more Teresa makes clear there must be an emptying of self. In the early Christian writers mentioned above the subject of how the soul encounters God had been much discussed. Most of these authors agree that some part of the human soul has the capacity to gaze upon God. Before it can do so, however, this part needs to be in a state of emptiness. It is this emptiness that God can fill with his own presence.

What does this state of emptiness involve? God who is encountered by the soul and in the soul is ineffable, and indescribable, far beyond human experience to know or grasp. In any encounter of God or experience of being filled by God, much of the range of ordinary human perception and thought has to be laid aside. The mind with its incessant activity has to be stilled and emptied. The spiritual journey involves many periods of darkness as one ceases from familiar modes of thought and perception. The will has to be stripped of much before it can be filled by divine light.

Teresa describes this transformation of the will in detail as no one before her had done. The person whose will has journeyed to the center differs drastically from the person who had begun the journey. By its travelling into the inner mansions, the will approaches closer and closer to light and more and more light pervades the whole soul. Its intrinsic beauty is revealed both to the person and to others.

Biblical Parallels

Teresa describes an inner journey in which the will makes choices and is transformed. Can we find parallels in what Jesus says for this type of activity within the soul? Several parables suggest what seem to be similar ideas. In the parable of the *Prodigal Son* (Luke 15:11–32) we see the younger son free to make choices, both to leave the Father's house and to return. We see the elder son with freedom to have remained home and to refuse to welcome his brother home. In the story of the *Lost Sheep* (Luke 15:3–7) human beings can clearly go astray and be sought tenderly by God. In both stories the longing of God for us is very strong just as Teresa depicts God, at the center of each soul, profoundly loving us.

Jesus describes the kingdom of heaven as a "treasure hidden in a field" which, when found, demands the sacrifice of all that one has (Matt. 13:44). So too this kingdom resembles a "pearl of great value" that one sells all to buy (Matt. 13:45). The "treasure" and "pearl" are our soul. They are also the divine Guest who dwells at the center of our being. God occupies the innermost mansion of the castle and is our most valued possession. We are to give up all in our quest for God. "Where our treasure is, so is our heart" (Matt. 6:21). Our dearest treasure is to be found in our heart or soul itself.

But how are we to find this treasure? Jesus tells us: "Whenever you pray, go into your room and shut the door and pray to your Father who is in secret" (Matt. 6:6). The "room" that Jesus mentions can be taken as the soul itself. We are to go inward, moving deeper and deeper into stillness and silence.

If we travel to the center of the soul, there we encounter God. The journey of our wills inward somehow allows the light of God's grace to flood the rest of our soul. This grace is in particular the love of God filling the soul and ravishing it. During the journey our wills become "empty" and "small." We learn again and again to "deny" ourselves, to take up our cross and to follow Jesus (Matt. 10:38). We seek the "narrow" gate and the "hard" road that lead to life (Matt. 7:14). In a way the will becomes as small as a "mustard seed" or a "few grains of yeast" (Matt. 13:31–33). But once these are placed in the right medium, they grow, flourish, and help others. So too the will, filled with God's love and grace, becomes rich in love for others.

Jesus suggests that he is the "vine" and we, the "branches." In him we "bear much fruit"; without him we "can do nothing" (John 15:5). When our wills are surrendered completely to the divine will, we "abide" in the love of Jesus (John 15:9). Jesus becomes the life of our souls. Then it is he, to whom our wills are surrendered, who loves in us. We can keep his commandment: "Love one another as I have loved you" (John 15:12).

Jesus calls us urgently to a life of prayer. "Ask, and it will be given you; search, and you will find; knock, and the door will be opened for you" (Matt. 7:7). He calls us to enter deep within where the kingdom of heaven is to be found. In the depths of our souls we will learn the truth he spoke in the last discourse: "I am in my Father, and you in me, and I in you" (John 14:20, cf. 17:23). Then what Jesus described will come true: "Those who love me will keep my word, and my Father will love them, and we will come to them and make our home with them" (John 14:23). At the center of our soul we encounter God, a trinity of persons; the Father, the Son, and the "Spirit of Truth" (John 14:17). To dwell in the innermost mansion is to be "sanctified in truth" (John 17:17). Then the love of the Father and of Jesus is in us (John 17:26) and in that love we can love others.

This journey involves in particular a choice of the will. God will never force us to come to himself in the center of our souls. We must choose to do so. We must open up to God. Jesus calls to us: "Listen! I am standing at the door, knocking; if you hear my voice and open the door, I will come in to you and eat with you, and you with me" (Rev. 3:20). For the person on the spiritual journey being "lukewarm" cannot be an option: Jesus does not approve of such individuals (Rev. 3:16). The treasure demands the sacrifice of all (Matt. 13:44). But the prize is beyond price: it is an encounter with God within.

"Immortal Diamond"

In this general overview of the *Interior Castle* we have seen Teresa describe the soul of each person as a palace made of diamond or crystal, having several rooms or mansions. In the center mansion God dwells, giving life to the soul and filling it with light. Because of the nature of this soul, all people are, in the core of their being, essentially beautiful and lovable.

With our free will we can affect the state of this soul within. Those who choose to dwell outside this palace, ignoring God and a holy way of life, cause the palace itself to be in darkness. Those who enter the palace encounter more and more light. At the end of this inner journey is God, the source of light and grace. The closer one travels to the center, the more the soul is filled with light.

Essential to this teaching on the soul by Teresa is one truth: every person is loved by God and is lovable. Not all souls are always beautiful. Human beings exhibit a wide range of positive and negative traits. Within each individual characteristics that are deserving of admiration and blame exist. Yet, basically, everyone's nature is precious. In order for the soul to exhibit its potential loveliness the will may have to undergo much transformation. Growth in self-knowledge can be painful. It may offer great challenges for change. It may demand sacrifices of people and things held dear. It may involve the loss of cherished ideas and ways of thinking.

Spiritual growth can be like travelling through a hall of mirrors. Each time a reflection is caught, the inadequacies and weaknesses of that reflection become apparent. The image must change again and again. One image alone will prove desirable; one image alone is to be cherished. This is the image of Jesus into whom we are being slowly transformed (2 Cor. 3:18). Despite, therefore, all that may be negative or ugly within ourselves we are potentially beautiful. We are also actually beautiful for the precious nature of the soul is the same in each of us.

Gerard Manly Hopkins in one of his poems speaks of the change that the resurrection will bring about, a change made possible because, just as Teresa also teaches, the human person is in essence precious and valuable:

> In a flash, at a trumpet crash,
> I am all at once what Christ is, since he was what I am, and
> This, Jack, joke, poor potsherd, patch, matchwood, immortal
> diamond,
> is immortal diamond.

Hopkins suggests that in his being he is nothing particularly admirable or special. He calls himself a "joke," a piece of broken pottery ("poor potsherd"), a "patch" of cloth, and a frail piece of wood ("matchwood"). This may be so but still, despite all this, he states that he is "immortal diamond." Nothing can change this fact. Heaven and paradise are for everyone and become possible because our souls, exquisitely beautiful, have been redeemed by Jesus.

According to Teresa, all human beings have this exquisitely beautiful "diamond" within. Having the awareness of our inner beauty can significantly alter our perception of ourselves and others. If we look out early on a winter morning to see a heavy frost upon the lawn, what do we behold? Drops of dew have been transformed into thousands and thousands of diamonds glinting and shining in the first light. This is how God beholds human beings. Teresa too, in her image of the soul, suggests that we are far more than the eye usually sees. To others we may appear to be simply human beings. Inwardly we are actually diamonds that can catch the divine light. Our souls make us wondrous jewels. How wonderful, therefore, the journey into the center of this jewel, the journey through the seven mansions! Through these mansions Teresa acts as our expert guide.

Notes

1. All translations, with minor editorial adjustments, are taken from *The Collected Works of St. Teresa of Avila*, trans. by K. Kavanaugh, OCD and O. Rodriguez, OCD (Washington, DC: ICS Publications, 1980), Vol. 2, with page references given.

2. Recent translations of the *Republic* include the following: G. M. A. Grube, revised by C. D. C. Reeve (Indianapolis: Hackett, 1992), R. W. Sterling and W. C. Scott (New York: Norton, 1985), and R. Waterfield (Oxford: Oxford Univ. Press, 1993).

3. Useful studies of these writers are: H. D. Egan, SJ, *Christian Mysticism* (New York: Pueblo, 1984), C. Jones, G. Wainwright, E. Yavold, SJ, ed., *The Study of Spirituality* (Oxford: Oxford Univ. Press, 1986), U. King, *Christian Mystics* (New York: Shuster and Shuster, 1998), A. E. McGrath, *Christian Spirituality: an Introduction* (Oxford: Blackwells, 1999), P. Pourrat, SS, trans. D. Attwater, *Christian Spirituality* (Westminster, MD: Newman Press, 1953–5), 4 volumes, J. Walsh, SJ, *Spirituality through the*

Centuries (London: Burns and Oates, 1964), R. Woods, OP, *Christian Spirituality* (Chicago: Thomas More Press, 1989), and, in particular, the three volumes by Bernard McGinn: *The Foundations of Mysticism* (New York; Crossroad, 1991), *The Growth of Mysticism* (New York: Crossroad, 1994), and *The Flowering of Mysticism* (New York: Crossroad, 1998).

4. See above note 2.

5. "That Nature is a Heraclitean Fire and of the Comfort of the Resurrection" in *God's Grandeur and Other Poems* (New York: Dover, 1995), 48–9.

2
Teresa of Avila:
Journey through the Soul

*We need no wings
to go in search of God
but need only to withdraw
into our hearts
where God waits for us.*

(*Way of Perfection*, 28.2)

Genesis teaches us that we are made in "the image of God." Exactly what in us constitutes this image has been a subject of much discussion over the centuries. Different aspects of the human being have been suggested: the very life within us, our capacity to think, to love, to express free choices of will. In the previous chapter we mentioned Teresa's references to the movement of the will through the mansions of the soul. In this current chapter we will focus first on the human being as made in the image of God. Second, we will trace out the elaborate stages of the journey by which the will comes to be united in love with the divine will. This journey culminates in the depths of the soul.

Why is it that the will moves into and through the mansions of the soul? Teresa pictures the will of each person as choosing its location within the soul. It can stay outside the castle altogether, focusing upon whatever fascinates it there. Or it can enter into the castle and begin its journey through the complex structure of the soul. It need not, and very likely may not, travel through all the mansions to the center where God dwells. But in everyone it may make some progress through certain mansions. Why does it make this journey?

The essential nature of the will is to love. During each life it is drawn to love dwelling in the seventh mansions. Love there constantly calls to the will: "Lo, I stand at the door and knock. If anyone hears me calling and opens the door, I will enter the house and have supper with that person and that person, with me" (Rev. 3:20). The will always has the capacity to love. According to Plato, as we saw earlier, it always loves and chooses what it considers to be good. But the objects of its love may vary in worthiness. As it journeys through the mansions, it learns slowly what to value, what to choose, and what to love.

The Bible teaches us what we are to love. "You shall love the Lord, your God, with all your heart, and with all your soul, and with all your strength" (Deut. 6:4). Jesus said: "You shall love the Lord your God with all your heart, with all your soul, with all your strength, and with all your mind, and your neighbor as yourself." In all the possible ways in which human beings may be made in the "image of God," our ability to love seems to be most important. Jesus says that we are to love God: with heart, soul, strength, and mind. Love is also to be poured forth to our neighbor in the same degree that we cherish ourselves.

Teresa teaches that when the will arrives at the seventh mansions, it will have learned to love perfectly both God and neighbor. There it will be identified with the divine will which only wills the good of each person. In its journey, the will, therefore, is transformed into love, suffused and altered by divine love.

We are all born with a particular soul. As the will journeys through its complicated structures, we come to know this soul and to know ourselves. Who we are at any moment is determined by where our will dwells within the soul. In the journey described by Teresa we also come to know more than ourselves. Within our own being there dwells one who has created us, who sustains us, redeems us, and who loves us. This wondrous guest of our soul becomes the object of our longing. Our wills come to love God within. "If anyone loves me, that person will keep my commandments and my Father and I will come to dwell within" (John 14:23).

Teresa teaches that our spiritual growth results from our travelling inward. Let us trace what she says about the journey of the will through the mansions of the soul. In the first to fourth mansions we can mention two topics: the state of the soul or will and the prayer it experiences. In the fifth to seventh mansions the soul or will at prayer becomes Teresa's chief topic.

First Mansions

Description. When we enter the first mansions, we are drawn inward by a basic longing for God. We try to avoid any serious sin. In our actions we try to imitate Jesus. There are many entrances to these first mansions since there is never a set way for all to travel to God. These first mansions are very diverse in nature with many entrances.

> Thus I say that you should think not in terms of just a few rooms but in terms of a million; for souls, all with good intentions, enter here in many ways. (293)

But the first mansions are not pleasant settings for the will. First of all, they are in a "darkened" state so that the light that pervades them is not noticed (294). The reason for the darkness is the "many bad things like snakes, vipers, and poisonous creatures that enter" along with the will (294). These unpleasant creatures are the affairs of the world that distract the attention of the will: "worldly things . . . possessions, honor, or business affairs" (294).

To allow the will to advance from these first mansions there will be need of growth in self-knowledge, something important for the whole journey (291–92). In particular one virtue is essential: humility, both to see who God is and who human beings are.

In the first mansions there will be opposition to progress because the devil is "like a noiseless file" (295). He likes to make good intentions excessive. People at the beginning of spiritual growth often lay out a challenging agenda for themselves. They plan activities that they judge to be holy. They strive to practice virtue in a rigorous and compelling way. They undertake good works in a number that may prove exhausting. They exhibit in excessive degree an "indiscreet zeal" (296).

As a consequence of all these measures people find that they cannot persevere. Soon they lose heart and give up any idea of striving for spiritual growth. What is abundantly apparent at the beginning of the spiritual journey is that people imagine that they can be in control. They think that by sheer effort of will they can become spiritual and holy. But it will not prove to be so. Good will is needed, to be sure. People must make a commitment to growth. Grace, however, is always necessary and it must be abundant.

Teresa says, therefore, that the devil tries hard to tempt people to excessive behavior at the very beginning of their inclination to "enter the castle" (293). If he proves successful, people may hasten out of the palace and stay happily there, all thought of spiritual growth discarded. Only the memory of a dismal failure of trying to be good may remain. The devil in the first mansions tempts people to excessive devotion. He also distorts their judgments of their own actions, making them believe that minor faults are serious offences. He leads such people likewise to judge others harshly. "Mutual love" (296) becomes difficult or absent.

We see that at the beginning of the spiritual journey, "much discretion is necessary" (296). Otherwise, the will may end up moving out of the castle instead of advancing further within it.

Nature of prayer. In the first mansions the will engages in some form of prayer. This prayer proves to be a prerequisite for entry: "The door of entry to this castle is prayer and reflection" (286). Teresa assumes that all prayer has an element of reflection in it. We must be aware of whom we are "speaking to," what we are "asking," and of whom (286). Clearly, at this stage, prayer is an encounter with God as the object of reverence and worship. Little of the light that comes from God within and pervades all mansions is even perceived. Certainly its origins are not recognized as yet. God may still seem to be a being outside the person, the distant object of all prayers and petition. People in these mansions have as yet no awareness that God dwells at the center of their souls, there to be worshipped and adored.

Second Mansions

Description. The will now is most eager to advance into the castle but it still lacks a firm resolve. On the one hand, it hears an irresistible voice:

> This Lord desires intensely that we love him and seek his company, so much so that from time to time he calls us to draw near him. (298)

On the other hand, the will meets many temptations that draw it back into the first mansions and even outside the castle.

> Certainly the soul undergoes great trials here. If the devil, especially, realizes that it has all it needs in temperament and habits to advance far, he will gather all hell together to make the soul go back outside. (300)

What proves helpful for people in the second mansions is conversation with those who have traveled further into the castle. The will must be determined to advance, trusting that sufficient grace for the journey will be given. In particular, the will must not hope for divine consolations. We are not to enter the castle to acquire anything for self but to find there the object of our love and to adore this divine being.

As we proceed, God helps the will in its journey and knows what experiences are best for us.

> His Majesty knows best what is suitable for us. There's no need for us to be advising him about what he

should give us, for he can rightly tell us that we don't know what we are asking for. (301)

In this stage of its journey, the will endures "falls" (302). But even these may prove helpful in teaching it how to advance. Teresa points out that people may encounter within themselves disharmony and discord. But peace has to come to reign among the inner faculties:

> Well, believe me, if we don't obtain and have peace in our own houses, we'll not find it outside. Let this war be ended. Through the blood he shed for us I ask those who have not begun to enter within themselves to do so; and those who have begun, not to let the war make them turn back. (302)

Gradually the inner conflict and distress lessen and the will can be brought back to "recollection" (302).

The journey ahead into the farther mansions is one filled by love. A faithful lover is calling:

> This true lover never leaves it, accompanying it and giving it life and being. (299)

But what is the cost of advancing? The soul suffers great fear. It dreads the loss of prestige, health, and close relationships with friends and relatives.

Teresa says that those in the first mansions are like the deaf who cannot hear the voice of God. Those in the second mansions, in contrast, begin to hear this voice:

> So these persons are able to hear the Lord when he calls. Since they are getting closer to where His Majesty dwells, he is a very good neighbor. His mercy and goodness are so bountiful; whereas we are occupied in our pastimes, business affairs, pleasures, and worldly buying and selling, and still falling into sin and rising again. (298)

Once the voice of God is heard, nothing else matters and "his voice is so sweet the poor soul dissolves at not doing immediately what he commands" (298).

These second mansions are still not very light. They have, however, more light than the first mansions and this light draws the will forward. The soul begins to sense that this light comes from a divine guest within.

Nature of prayer. Prayer is necessary for entry into the second mansions. Teresa emphasizes the necessity of "entering into ourselves" and "coming to know ourselves" (303). We are to reflect much on the life of Jesus (303). Our chief aim in prayer is to bring the "will into conformity with God's will" (301). At this stage God's will is for the soul to grow in virtue. Prayer will help this growth. This prayer may still be at an immature stage but it will always have in it the essential element of recollection. The soul becomes quiet in the presence of God and learns to listen for God's voice.

Third Mansions

Description. These mansions provide new challenge for the will. It has to learn not to trust in its own strength. It has already acquired discipline and prudence. It performs penance and acts of charity (306). But on its journey the will now begins to encounter more serious difficulties, to which Teresa refers:

> Since we are continually walking and are tired (for, believe me, it is a wearisome journey), we will be doing quite well if we don't go astray. (312)

The worst suffering in these mansions is that of aridity. Teresa urges that, when we experience dryness in prayer, we focus on humility (307). She suggests that God withdraws his grace for a little while so that we experience our limitations. Awareness of these limitations teaches us humility. In these mansions we learn what we are attached to by our reaction to their loss

(310–11). If we cannot bear the loss of wealth or honor, or endure some bodily suffering, we are clearly attached. In these mansions we learn something of self-renunciation. What our will may wish, it cannot always have. Even our carefully ordered spiritual life is disrupted so that our reason is not allowed to dominate. We are taught that we are not in control.

The negative experiences in these mansions can discourage people and make them hesitate to continue on their journey within. But this must not be allowed to happen.

> Enter, enter, my daughters, into the interior rooms; pass on from your little works. By the mere fact that you are Christians you must do all these things and much more. It is enough for you to be God's vassals; don't let your desire be for so much that as a result you will be left with nothing. Behold the saints who entered this king's chamber, and you will see the difference between them and us. Don't ask for what you have not deserved, nor should it enter our minds that we have merited this favor however much we may have served—we who have offended God. (307)

Perseverance is essential and eagerness to press on. People must not assume that aridity and inner sufferings are simply signs of "imperfection" (309). Such imperfection may contribute to inner trials but these trials may be God's way of purifying the soul. They must be nobly born. The solution always will be to strive for more and more humility:

> Humility is the ointment for our wounds because if we indeed have humility, even though there may be a time of delay, the surgeon, who is our Lord, will come to heal us. (311)

All, however, is not darkness in these mansions because God sends us spiritual sweetness to encourage us:

> But in these rooms of which we're speaking, the Lord, as one who is just or even merciful, does not fail to

pay; for he always gives much more than we deserve
by giving us consolations far greater than those we
find in the comforts and distractions of life. (313)

One truth is important to grasp:

Perfection as well as its reward does not consist in
spiritual delights but in greater love and in deeds done
with greater justice and truth. (313)

More and more attention has to be given to growing in love for
God and for neighbor.

In these mansions the will starts to be transformed but its love
is still much filled with fear (312). The will is learning to love but
it is not a love of full surrender that will come later. At this time, it
is a love in which "reason is still very much in control" (312). The
will yearns for God but acts cautiously. Its generosity and
response are as yet guarded and not marked by full abandon.
Teresa's advice is firm:

Since we are so circumspect, everything offends us
because we fear everything; so we don't dare go
further—as if we could reach these dwelling places
while leaving to other persons the trouble of treading
the path for us. Since this is not possible, let us exert
ourselves, my sisters, for the love of the Lord; let's
abandon our reason and our fears into his hands; let's
forget this natural weakness that can take up our
attention so much. (312)

Only a lack of humility will keep us from travelling farther
forward.

Nature of prayer. In these mansions, the will engages in
"periods of recollection" (306). Teresa does not give specific
details of the prayer occurring in these mansions but one truth is
clear: during aridity people must still pray. In these mansions too
meditation is important. Such meditation will involve the use of
all faculties: intellect, memory, and imagination. With these we

ponder on Scripture and on aspects of the spiritual life, such as the practice of virtue or good works. Teresa calls on us to reflect also on the trials we receive. This reflection will lead to valuable self-knowledge (310). Only with such knowledge can people advance farther in their spiritual journey. Only a sense of humility will cause a strong feeling of gratitude to abide in the heart. In these mansions God may from time to time grant special favors to the soul. These will help the soul to praise. Such favors

> come brimming over with love and fortitude by which you can journey with less labor and grow in the practice of works and virtues. (314)

Both darkness and light in prayer are part of God's way of drawing the soul further inward.

Fourth Mansions

Description. In the first three sets of rooms or mansions, God gently and quietly invites the will forward. In the remaining four sets of rooms God gives particular help for the journey. Now the gifts of the Holy Spirit are poured forth. Now the will comes to surrender more and more to God summoning it within. Supernatural elements of spiritual life enter. It is no longer the efforts of the person that prove crucial. In the fourth mansions we learn in much more detail how God works on the will. In these mansions we begin to see the distinction that exists between the mind or imagination and the will. Teresa makes it clear that it is the will that is crucial for spiritual growth. The principal aim of this will is to learn always to choose love:

> The important thing is not to think much but to love much. (319)

God's gift in these mansions of the soul is infused prayer or the "prayer of quiet." Teresa had spoken of this type of prayer in her

Life but she now says that she has acquired a deeper understanding of this wonderful gift from God. To describe it she uses
the image of water. On the one hand, people can draw water with
difficulty and labor. This parallels the spiritual life of the first
three mansions. On the other hand, however, the source of water
can be found "right there . . . there is no need of any skill . . .
water is always flowing from the spring" (323). This water is like
the infused prayer or "prayer of quiet" of the fourth mansions.
What happens? A gift of prayer is bestowed upon the will, which
deeply enjoys this gift. While this is occurring, the mind may
engage in tumultuous and ceaseless activity:

> Ordinarily the mind flies about quickly, for only God
> can hold it fast in such a way as to make it seem that
> we are somehow loosed from this body. (319)

The faculties of the soul can be "occupied and recollected in
God" while the mind can be "distracted" (320). Teresa
profoundly understands the division that can be found within
the soul. People need a depth of self-understanding to grasp
what is happening in their souls in these fourth mansions.

> Terrible trials are suffered because we don't under-
> stand ourselves, and that which isn't bad at all but
> good we think is a serious fault. This lack of knowl-
> edge causes the afflictions of many people who
> engage in prayer: complaints about interior trials, at
> least to a great extent, by people who have no
> learning; melancholy and loss of health; and even the
> complete abandonment of prayer. For such persons
> don't reflect that there is an interior world here within
> us. Just as we cannot stop the movement of the
> heavens, but they proceed in rapid motion, so neither
> can we stop our mind; and then the faculties of the
> soul go with it, and we think we are lost and have
> wasted the time spent before God. But the soul is
> perhaps completely joined with him in the dwelling
> places very close to the center while the mind is on the

outskirts of the castle suffering from a thousand wild
and poisonous beasts, and meriting by this suffering.
As a result we should not be disturbed; nor should we
abandon prayer, which is what the devil wants us to
do. For the most part all the trials and disturbances
come from our not understanding ourselves. (320)

In this passage Teresa distinguishes clearly between the state
of the will and that of the mind. The will receives an infusion of
the presence of God. It must resist any temptation of following
the activity of the mind and simply rest in its gift. Teresa says of
herself:

For all this turmoil in my head doesn't hinder prayer
or what I am saying, but the soul is completely taken
up in its quiet, love, desires, and clear knowledge.
(321)

But this rest is not easy to sustain. The soul can be greatly
disturbed by the ceaseless activity of the mind, however much it
desires "rest and tranquility" (321). Such inner turmoil is
distressing but there is hope if the will continues its journey.

So, Lord, bring us to the place where these miseries
will not taunt us, for they seem sometimes to be
making fun of the soul. Even in this life, the Lord frees
the soul from these miseries when it reaches the last
dwelling place. (321)

In describing the fourth mansions Teresa uses the image of
two water troughs. In the case of one, water from distant aqueducts has to fill it. In the case of the other, water comes from a
source of water "right there" (323). Teresa compares consolations received from meditation to this first water trough. This
meditation depends largely on our own efforts. Our intellects are
involved and we use various creatures to help in the meditation.

The second water trough resembles consolations sent directly
by God.

With this other fount, the water comes from its own source which is God. And since His Majesty desires to do so—when he is pleased to grant some supernatural favor—he produces this delight with the greatest peace and quiet and sweetness in the very interior part of ourselves. I don't know from where or how, nor is that happiness and delight experienced, as are earthly consolations, in the heart. I mean there is no similarity at the beginning, for afterward the delight fills everything; this water overflows through all the dwelling places and faculties until reaching the body. That is why I said that it begins in God and ends in ourselves. (324)

This wondrous consolation arises from the depths of our beings.

It seems that since heavenly water begins to arise from this spring I'm mentioning that is deep within us, it swells and expands our whole interior being, producing ineffable blessings; nor does the soul even understand what is given to it there. It perceives a fragrance, let us say for now, as though there were in that interior depth a brazier giving off sweet-smelling perfumes. (324)

This consolation is not the result of the activity of our minds or imaginations. It is totally a gift.

This spiritual delight is not something that can be imagined, because however diligent our efforts we cannot acquire it. The very experience of it makes us realize that it is not of the same metal as we ourselves but fashioned from the purest gold of the divine wisdom. Here, in my opinion, the faculties are not united but absorbed and looking as though in wonder at what they see. (325)

God pours consolations into the soul when and where he wishes. These consolations are not deserved nor are we to strive for them (326). When they occur, we are to remain humble and detached (327). The effects of this type of prayer are many. First, the soul is enlarged:

> This interior sweetness and expansion can be verified in the fact that the soul is not tied down as it was before in things pertaining to the service of God, but has much more freedom. (332)

It is now eager for the works of God with a newfound freedom. It lacks fear of trials that may come. It sees that earthly things have much less value than before. It is strengthened in virtues.

> In sum, there is an improvement in all virtues. It will continue to grow if it doesn't turn back now to offending God; because if it does, then everything will be lost however high on the summit the soul may be. Nor should it be understood that if God grants this favor once or twice to a soul all these good effects will be caused. It must persevere in receiving them, for in this perseverance lies all our good. (332)

God has proved that he wants to be our "friend" (333). The will must now be strong in persevering.

Nature of prayer. What is infused prayer? Teresa mentions two types of prayer in her discussion. Recollection precedes infused prayer and is of a different type:

> The prayer of recollection is much less intense than the prayer of spiritual delight from God that I mentioned. But it is the beginning through which one goes to the other; for in the prayer of recollection, meditation, or the work of the intellect, must not be set aside. (331)

Recollection describes this type of prayer that a person actively chooses. In it meditation with the intellect forms an essential part. As mentioned above, this prayer is like water brought by aqueducts to fill a water trough.

Infused prayer, in contrast, is a total gift from God. The intellect or mind may carry on its own activity or it may come under God's influence.

> When His Majesty desires the intellect to stop, he occupies it in another way and gives it a light so far above what we can attain that it remains absorbed. Then, without knowing how, the intellect is much better instructed than it was through all the soul's efforts not to make use of it. Since God gave us our faculties that we might work with them and in this work they find their reward, there is no reason to charm them; we should let them perform their task until God appoints them to another greater one. (330)

Infused prayer is like water simply filling a water trough and even enlarging the trough as it fills it (331). In this type of prayer God's action dominates in the will:

> The will has such deep rest in its God that the clamor of the intellect is a terrible bother to it. There is no need to pay any attention to this clamor, for doing so would make the will lose much of what it enjoys. But one should leave the intellect go and surrender oneself into the arms of love, for His Majesty will teach the soul what it must do at that point. (331)

The mind cannot understand what is happening and should not strive to grasp the nature of this experience.

This infused prayer never lasts for a long time. The soul does not fall into a sleep. There is neither languor in this state nor any lack of consciousness of God. Instead, the soul feels great joy at being so close to God. This experience does not extend to the body or produce any exterior sensation. Infused prayer comes unexpectedly.

> It is given only to whom God wills to give it and often
> when the soul is least thinking of it. (326)

This prayer leads the will onward in its journey to God. Slowly it is learning how to surrender to the action of God within. The will comes to recognize its essential nature and its relationship with God:

> We belong to him . . . Let him do whatever he likes
> with us, bring us wherever he pleases. (326)

In these fourth mansions the will has advanced far toward God at the center of the soul. In the fifth to seventh mansions, however, it will make much greater progress. It is these mansions that Teresa describes in great detail. With regard to them we learn most about the exquisite nature of the soul that is found in each human being.

Fifth Mansions

The soul and prayer. In the fifth mansions there are "riches and treasures and delights" (335). We dig for the "precious pearl of contemplation" (336) in ourselves and thus, to some extent, enjoy heaven on earth. But to receive such a gift we must give all. Here, as in the fourth mansions, God pours infused prayer into the will. When the will receives this prayer, the faculties are completely at rest. The mind has no power to think. In loving, the will is unaware of what it loves. In desiring, it does not know what it desires. In this state the will

> is like one who in every respect has died to the world
> so as to live completely in God. (336)

Before, in the fourth mansions, the will had doubts about the experience of infused prayer. It wondered whether the experience came from God or from the devil. Now it is sure of its divine source. The memory, imagination, and understanding are not in any way an obstacle to the grace that God now pours into the soul. He does not allow our thoughts to understand his gift nor in any way to impede it:

> The soul is left with such wonderful blessings because God works within it without anyone disturbing him, not even ourselves. What will he not give, who is so fond of giving and who can give all that he wants? (338)

The devil is helpless, being incapable of understanding what is going on.

The period of this prayer is always short but the soul is sure that it has experienced union with God:

> For during the time of this union it neither sees, nor hears, nor understands, because the union is always short and seems to the soul even shorter than it probably is. God so places himself in the interior of that soul that when it returns to itself it can in no way doubt that it was in God and God was in it. (339)

> In this state the will "has been entirely surrendered to him." (340)

Teresa then presents her wonderful image of the silkworm. That worm spins a cocoon, buries itself within it, and in time emerges as a beautiful white butterfly. The soul too is to "hide its life in Christ" (Col. 3:3) by acts of prayer, penance, obedience, and all good works and also by being free of self-love, self-will, and attachments. The will must, in a way, "die" so that it can come to gaze upon God. It will be completely hidden in the greatness of God, just as happens to the silkworm:

> The silkworm, which is fat and ugly, then dies, and a little white butterfly, which is very pretty, comes forth from the cocoon. (342)

In the same way in which silkworm becomes a butterfly, the
will in this infused prayer becomes truly "dead to the world"
(343). It has done the work of spinning the cocoon.

> Therefore, courage, my daughters! Let's be quick to do
> this work and weave this little cocoon by getting rid of
> our self-love and self-will, our attachment to any
> earthly thing, and by performing deeds of penance,
> prayer, mortification, obedience, and of all other
> things you know. Would to heaven that we would do
> what we know we must; and we are instructed about
> what we must do. Let it die; let this silkworm die, as it
> does in completing what it was created to do! And you
> will see how we see God, as well as ourselves placed
> inside his greatness, as is this little silkworm within
> its cocoon. (343)

Now, within the "cocoon," lost in God, it can be changed by
the action of divine grace.

The will that is making its journey to God is transformed. Its
only desire is to praise God, to suffer for God, and to bring all to
know God. It is completely detached from possessions, relationships, and all earthly things. But even now "it is not entirely
surrendered to God's will" (345), however much it strives for
this.

There is one great suffering that occurs in these mansions: an
overwhelming longing for the salvation of other souls. The soul
now suffers greatly over those who do not honor Jesus. As the
will draws nearer to God at the center of the soul, it becomes
acutely aware of how others honor or fail to honor him.

Teresa makes clear the state of this will as it abides in the fifth
mansions:

> Since that soul now surrenders itself into his hands
> and its great care makes it so surrendered that it
> neither knows nor wants anything more than what he
> wants for her . . . he desires that, without its under-
> standing how, it may go forth from this union

impressed with his seal. For indeed the soul does no more in this union than does the wax when another impresses a seal on it . . . Oh, goodness of God; everything must be at a cost to you! All you want is our will and that there be no impediment in the wax. (346)

The greatest need in these mansions is for the will to be surrendered to the will of God. Hindrances to this surrender of the will arise from "self-love, self-esteem, judging one's neighbors (even though in little things), a lack of charity for them, and not loving them as ourselves" (350). To die to self-will comes at a cost, but our will is to become one with God's will.

Nonetheless, take careful note, daughters, that it is necessary for the silkworm to die, and, moreover, at a cost to yourselves. In the delightful union, the experience of seeing oneself in so new a life greatly helps one to die; in the other union, it's necessary that, while living in this life, we ourselves put the silkworm to death. I confess this latter death will require a great deal of effort, or more than that; but it has its value. Thus if you come out victorious the reward will be much greater. But there is no reason to doubt the possibility of this death any more than that of true union with the will of God. This union with God's will is the union I have desired all my life; it is the union I ask the Lord for always and the one that is clearest and safest. (350)

In the fifth mansions, we come to grasp what God's will is for us. This knowledge is a great gift, since so often in life we may long to know God's will and be perplexed concerning its nature.

What do you think his will is, daughters? That we be completely perfect. See what we lack to be one with him and his Father as His Majesty asked. (350)

Such union of our will and the divine will finds expressions, in particular, in a perfect love of neighbor.

In describing what happens to the will in these mansions, Teresa uses imagery related to marriage. In the fifth mansions there occurs a "betrothal" of the will with God.

> You've already often heard that God espouses souls spiritually. Blessed be his mercy that wants so much to be humbled! And even though the comparison may be a coarse one I cannot find another that would better explain what I mean than the sacrament of marriage. This spiritual espousal is different in kind from marriage, for in these matters that we are dealing with there is never anything that is not spiritual. Corporal things are far distant from them, and the spiritual joys the Lord gives when compared to the delights married people must experience are a thousand leagues distant. For it is all a matter of love united with love, and the actions of love are most pure and so extremely delicate and gentle that there is no way of explaining them, but the Lord knows how to make them clearly felt. (354)

During this period of "betrothal" both God and the soul have a period of time to get to know each other.

> It seems to me that the prayer of union does not yet reach the stage of spiritual betrothal. Here below when two people are to be engaged, there is discussion about whether they are alike, whether they love each other, and whether they might meet together so as to become more satisfied with each other. So, too, in the case of this union with God, the agreement has been made, and this soul is well informed about the goodness of her spouse and determined to do his will in everything and in as many ways as she sees might make him happy. And His Majesty, as one who understands clearly whether these things about his betrothed are so, is happy with her. As a result he grants this mercy, for he desired her to know him

more and that they might meet together, as they say, and be united. We can say that union is like this, for it passes in a very short time. In it there no longer takes place the exchanging of gifts, but the soul sees secretly who this spouse is that she is going to accept. Through the work of the senses and the faculties she couldn't in any way or in a thousand years understand what she understands here in the shortest time. But being who he is, the spouse from that meeting alone leaves her more worthy for the joining of hands, as they say. The soul is left so much in love that it does for its part all it can to avoid disturbing this divine betrothal. But if it is careless about placing its affection in something other than him, it loses everything. And the loss is as great as the favors he was granting her, and cannot be exaggerated. (355)

The will must always strive to advance, ever fighting the temptation to self-love. This self-love will draw it away from God and prevent it from surrendering to him. If self-love is not checked, the will may lose its chance to progress further toward God.

Sixth Mansions

The soul and prayer. Of this part of the journey of the will Teresa writes most fully in the *Interior Castle* (11 chapters). These mansions are both terrible and wonderful. In them the will faces its most difficult challenges. It is in these mansions, "where the soul is now wounded with love for its spouse and strives for more opportunities to be alone and, in conformity with its state, to rid itself of everything that can be an obstacle to this solitude" (359). Teresa continues the imagery of marriage: the soul longs for betrothal and "is fully determined to take no other spouse" (359). The divine spouse, however, does not allow a full betrothal to occur because he wants the yearnings of the soul to become

even deeper. At this time suffering in various forms comes into a
person's life.

> Indeed, sometimes I reflect and fear that if a soul
> knew beforehand, its natural weakness would find it
> most difficult to have the determination to suffer and
> pass through these trials, no matter what blessings
> were represented to it—unless it had arrived at the
> seventh dwelling place. For once it has arrived there,
> the soul fears nothing and is absolutely determined to
> overcome every obstacle for God. And the reason is
> that it is always so closely joined to His Majesty that
> from this union comes its fortitude. I believe it will be
> well to recount some of those trials I know one will
> certainly undergo. Perhaps not all souls will be led
> along this path, although I doubt very much that
> those persons who sometimes enjoy so truly the
> things of heaven will live free of earthly trials that
> come in one way or another. (360)

These trials that the soul endures may be varied. It may be
blamed or, in contrast, falsely praised. It may endure physical
illness. There may be severe interior trials and all these the soul
must endure patiently.

> In sum, there is no remedy in this tempest but to wait
> for the mercy of God. For at an unexpected time, with
> one word alone or a chance happening, he so quickly
> calms the storm that it seems there had not been even
> as much as a cloud in that soul, and it remains filled
> with sunlight and much more consolation. And like
> one who has escaped from a dangerous battle and
> been victorious, it comes out praising our Lord; for it
> was he who fought for the victory. It knows very
> clearly that it did not fight, for all the weapons with
> which it could have defended itself are seen to be, it
> seems, in the hands of its enemies. Thus, it knows

clearly its wretchedness and the very little we of ourselves can do if the Lord abandons us. (364)

In these interior trials people feel that they have lost God altogether. Nothing that before served to have positive value for spiritual growth seems to avail at all now. The soul seems to be totally lost and to be forsaken by God. But the farther away God seems, the closer he actually is.

> Well then, what will this poor soul do when the torment goes on for many days? If it prays, it feels as though it hasn't prayed—as far as consolation goes, I mean. For consolation is not admitted into the soul's interior, nor is what one recites to oneself, even though vocal, understood. As for mental prayer, this definitely is not the time for that, because the faculties are incapable of the practice; rather, solitude causes greater harm—and also another torment for this soul is that it be with anyone or that others speak to it. And thus however much it forces itself not to do so, it goes about with a gloomy and ill-tempered mien that is externally very noticeable.
>
> Is it true that it will know how to explain its experiences? They are indescribable, for they are spiritual afflictions and sufferings that one cannot name. The best remedy (I don't mean for getting rid of them, because I don't find any, but so that they may be endured) is to engage in external works of charity and to hope in the mercy of God who never fails those who hope in him. May he be forever blessed, amen. (365)

In all this suffering God is still at work. These trials are to teach "the little dove" to "fly higher still" (366). Before God belongs entirely to the soul "he makes it desire him vehemently by certain delicate means the soul itself does not understand . . . There are impulses so delicate and refined, for they proceed from very deep within the interior part of the soul, that I don't know any comparison that will fit" (367).

How does God work on the soul? He suddenly, delectably wounds it: "His action is as quick as a falling comet" (367). The soul recognizes that "the wound is something precious, and it would never want to be cured" (367). What is happening is that the beloved, dwelling in the seventh mansions, is calling. When this occurs, all within is still: senses, imagination, and various faculties. The experience of the wound may be long or short. It is both painful and delightful. "The wound satisfies it much more than the delightful and painless absorption of the prayer of quiet" (367). What is acting upon the soul is love.

Teresa introduces an image of fire to explain what happens in the soul at this time.

> This action of love is so powerful that the soul dissolves with desire, and yet it doesn't know what to ask for since clearly it thinks that its God is with it.
>
> You will ask me: Well, if it knows this, what does it desire or what pains it? What greater good does it want? I don't know. I do know that it seems this pain reaches to the soul's very depths and that when he who wounds it draws out the arrow, it indeed seems, in accord with the deep love the soul feels, that God is drawing these very depths after him. I was thinking now that it's as though, from this fire enkindled in the brazier that is my God, a spark leapt forth and so struck the soul that the flaming fire was felt by it. And since the spark was not enough to set the soul on fire, and the fire is so delightful, the soul is left with that pain; but the spark merely by touching the soul produces that effect. It seems to me this is the best comparison I have come up with. This delightful pain—and it is not pain—is not continuous, although sometimes it lasts a long while; at other times it goes away quickly. This depends on the way the Lord wishes to communicate it, for it is not something that can be procured in any human way. But even though it sometimes lasts for a long while, it comes and goes.

> To sum up, it is never permanent. For this reason it doesn't set the soul on fire; but just as the fire is about to start, the spark goes out and the soul is left with the desire to suffer again that loving pain the spark causes. (368)

In these sixth mansions God can also speak to the soul. Teresa deals extensively with various types of locutions that the soul may experience. Those truly from God will bring great peace to the soul and remove all fear. They remain for a long time in the memory bringing certitude, hope, and delight. When God thus addresses the soul, "the very spirit that speaks puts a stop to all other thoughts and makes the soul attend to what is said" (378). Teresa says of this state of the soul:

> For he who was able to stop the sun . . . can make the faculties and the whole interior stop in such a way that the soul sees clearly that another greater Lord than itself governs that castle. (378)

Referring once again to the soul as a butterfly, Teresa says that all the longings of its will are for union with its spouse. God grants immense knowledge of himself to urge the will on. He gives some awareness of the kingdom that the will is coming to possess. This experience can be one of extreme ecstasy, which greatly affects the will:

> But it will happen that even though the extreme ecstasy ends, the will remains so absorbed and the intellect so withdrawn, for a day and even days, that the latter seems incapable of understanding anything that doesn't lead to awakening the will to love; and the will is wide awake to this love and asleep to becoming attached to any creature. (384)

The will comes to wish only what God wants, even though in its life it may be suffering much persecution and insult from others.

The will therefore experiences great ecstasy. Teresa refers again to the image of water and describes what effects appear in the soul.

> It seems the trough of water we mentioned . . . filled so easily and gently, I mean without any movement. Here this great God, who holds back the springs of water and doesn't allow the sea to go beyond its boundaries, lets loose the springs from which the water in this trough flows. With a powerful impulse, a huge wave arises up so forcefully that it lifts high this little bark that is our soul. A bark cannot prevent the furious waves from leaving it where they will; nor does the pilot have the power, nor do those who take part of the soul stay where it will or make its senses or faculties do other than what they are commanded; here the soul doesn't care what happens in the exterior senses. (387)

As a result, within the soul are left three effects: knowledge of the grandeur of God; self-knowledge and humility at the human condition; little regard for earthly things except for those used to serve God (390). The soul now yearns deeply for God.

> Even if it wanted to, it could not really desire anything else but to abandon itself into God's hands. (392)

> God gives these souls the strongest desire not to displease him in anything, however small, and the desire to avoid if possible every imperfection. (392)

At the same time the soul wishes also to serve his people. Teresa elaborates on the types of prayer that may occur as the will moves through these sixth mansions. Sometimes visions occur but the will is not to focus on these. The prayer may be lofty and ecstatic but the soul must always stay in close contact with the humanity of Christ, however sublime its prayer. Teresa insists that this contact is essential at all times. She asserts that "the further a soul advances the more it is accompanied by the good

Jesus" (405). She compares the presence of Jesus within the soul to that of a precious stone in a reliquary:

> Within the soul the Lord is present. It is as though we had in a gold vessel a precious stone having the highest value and curative powers. We know very certainly that it is there although we have never seen it . . . But we dare not look at it or open the reliquary, nor can we, because the manner of opening this reliquary is known solely by the one to whom the jewel belongs. Even though he lent us the jewel for our own benefit, he has kept the key to the reliquary and will open it, as something belonging to him when he desires to show us the contents, and he will take the jewel back when he wants to, as he does. (411)

Jesus, therefore, is the great treasure within the soul. He must remain the "way" for the will as it continues its spiritual journey.

In her final chapter on the sixth mansions (11), Teresa elaborates further on God's making himself present in the soul. The experience resembles a fire, a blow, or a wound in the deepest part of the soul. The will is being utterly stripped; its entire longing is centered only for God.

> On fire with this thirst, it cannot get to the water; and the thirst is not one that is endurable but already at such a point that nothing will take it away. Nor does the soul desire that the thirst be taken away save by that water of which our Lord spoke to the Samaritan woman. Yet no one gives such water to the soul. (423–24)

The will must have great courage to persevere in these trials as God makes himself known. The hope for the next mansions makes it possible to endure all that occurs in the sixth mansions.

> Oh, God help me! Lord, how you afflict your lovers! But everything is small in comparison with what you give them afterward. It's natural that what is worth

much costs much. Moreover, if the suffering is to purify the soul so that it might enter the seventh dwelling place—just as those who will enter heaven must be cleansed in purgatory—it is as small as a drop of water in the sea. Furthermore, in spite of all this torment and affliction, which cannot be surpassed, I believe, by any earthly afflictions (for this person has suffered many bodily as well as spiritual pains, but they all seemed nothing in comparison with this suffering), the soul feels that the pain is so precious—it understands very well—that one could not deserve it. However, this awareness is not of a kind that alleviates the suffering in any way. But with this knowledge, the soul suffers the pain very willingly and would suffer it all its life, if God were to be thereby served; although the soul would not then die once but be always dying, for truly the suffering is no less than death. (424)

Seventh Mansions

The soul and God. The journey of the will ends in the seventh mansions. Here it finds the light that it has sought for so long.

When our Lord is pleased to have pity on this soul that he has already as his spouse because of what it suffered through its desires, he brings it, before the spiritual marriage is consummated, into his dwelling place which is this seventh. For just as in heaven so in the soul His Majesty must have a room where he dwells alone. Let us call it another heaven. (428)

In the sixth mansions the soul did not understand the nature of its encounter with God. In the seventh mansions, in contrast, "the soul understands as a most profound truth that all Three Persons are one substance and one power and one knowledge and are God alone" (430). The experience of God becomes one of companionship that varies in intensity but is ever present. The soul now is ever with God and is ever more committed to the service of God:

> You may think that as a result the soul will be outside itself and so absorbed that it will be unable to be occupied with anything else. On the contrary, the soul is much more occupied than before with everything pertaining to the service of God; and once its duties are over it remains with that enjoyable company. If the soul does not fail God, he will never fail, in my opinion, to make his presence clearly known to it. It has strong confidence that since God has granted this favor he will not allow it to lose the favor. Though the soul thinks this, it goes about with greater care than ever not to displease him in anything. (430–31)

Teresa carries on the image of spiritual marriage, emphasizing that now the will and God become truly united. This is a stage of greater union than that of spiritual betrothal. The will and God are like rain that has joined with a river, the water of a stream with that of the sea, or two beams of light that have become one. Now the will, the little butterfly, dies and it does so "with the greatest joy because its life is now Christ" (435). In its earthly life the soul serves God who sustains it. The will has been entirely stripped:

> For it is very certain that in emptying ourselves of all that is creature and detaching ourselves from it for the love of God, the same Lord will fill us with himself. (436)

The seventh mansions are the final destination of the will. It has come to dwell in the center of the soul which is truly a "heaven":

> The Lord puts the soul in this dwelling of his, which is the center of the soul itself. They say that the empyreal

heaven where the Lord is does not move as do the other heavens; similarly, it seems, in the soul that enters here there are none of those movements that usually take place in the faculties and the imagination and do harm to the soul, nor do these stirrings take away its peace. (436)

The will in the center is at peace but all the faculties may not be in this state:

It should not be thought that the faculties, senses, and passions are always in this peace; the soul is, yes. But in those other dwelling places, times of war, trial, and fatigue are never lacking; however, they are such that they do not take the soul from its place and its peace; that is, as a rule. (437)

Nothing can draw the will from the seventh mansions: it has made a firm choice to stay. There it has found God whom it endlessly adores.

The whole focus of the person is now on service of God and acceptance of his divine will. Most importantly there is "forgetfulness of self" (438). Trials and afflictions may come but great peace and inner joy exist in the center of the soul. No longer are there raptures but only abiding peace in the embrace of God. What the soul experiences is "prayer of union" (441). In this state the will is detached from all that is not God:

There is a great detachment from everything and a desire to be always either alone or occupied in something that will benefit some soul. There are no interior trials or feelings of dryness, but the soul lives with a remembrance and tender love of our Lord. It would never want to go without praising him. When it becomes distracted the Lord himself awakens it in the manner mentioned, for one sees most clearly that that impulse, or I don't know what to call the feeling, proceeds from the interior depths of the soul, as was said of the impulses in the previous dwelling place. Here, in this dwelling place, these impulses are experienced most gently, but they do not proceed from the mind or the memory, nor do they come from anything that would make one think the soul did something on its own. This experience is an ordinary and frequent one, for it has been observed carefully. Just as a fire does not shoot its flames downward but upward, however great a fire is enkindled, so one experiences here that this interior movement proceeds from the center of the soul and awakens the faculties. (440)

The will now, totally conformed to God's will, engages joyfully in good works and bears much fruit. God's purpose in bringing the will into the seventh mansions is to make it like Jesus and for "the birth always of good works" (446). Teresa says that ideally Martha and Mary must be joined:

> Believe me, Martha and Mary must join together in order to show hospitality to the Lord and have him always present and not host him badly by failing to give him something to eat. How would Mary, always seated at his feet, provide him with food if her sister did not help her? His food is that in every way possible we draw souls that they may be saved and praise him always. (448)

The contemplative soul will be truly a person of prayer in action. Inwardly, the will is caught up in God. Outwardly, the person does frequent good works, pouring forth love that flows from within. The person has become an image of Jesus, praying and loving.

The Whole Journey

We have traced the journey of the will through the mansions of the soul. As our description has shown, Teresa uses different images to give details of the journey. Most important is that of the butterfly since it relates directly to the will. The silkworm spins a cocoon, enters within, and emerges as a lovely white butterfly. In a similar way the will is transformed as it moves through the mansions and grows spiritually. But, as we have seen, the butterfly does not live. It dies as does the will when it becomes identified with the will of God: "You have died, and your life is hidden with Christ in God" (Col. 3:3). Then the person can say with Saint Paul: "Anyone united to the Lord becomes one spirit with him" (1 Cor. 6:17). This person can likewise claim: "I have been crucified with Christ; and it is no longer I who live, but it is Christ who lives in me" (Gal. 2:19–20).

If we look to our own experiences, to what can we compare the journey of the will that Teresa describes? One example would be as follows. The first to the third mansions are like a walk up to a beautiful church set on a hill. To arrive there we need to climb vigorously. We practice discipline and self-control. We are drawn upward and see only this church as our goal. It is nightfall when we arrive at the church.

Parallel to the fourth mansions is the state of the will now beholding this church that is lit from within. The evening causes the wondrous stained glass windows to be fully visible from outside. On some, figures appear. On others, abstract patterns whirl out in a wide range of colors. The windows can be said to represent the life of each person. The figures on them are the people in our lives, some close relations, others, acquaintances. The colored pieces of glass in different patterns represent all the circumstances of our daily lives. How clear and vivid the windows appear, shining forth to the darkness without!

In this situation, parallel to the fourth mansions, we discern clearly the people and events that make up our lives. From all we must become detached, both from relationships and circumstances. Our goal must in some ways be God alone. We are to serve others but not be attached to any persons in particular.

Now, as in the fifth mansions, the will moves inward. It enters the church, richly illumined by lights within. Here, because it is evening, the figures and patterns of the stained glass windows are no longer visible! Gradually the inner light fades and we become aware of one light only: the red glow of the tabernacle light. Jesus becomes our one and only focus.

And then, as in the sixth mansions, we enter into complete darkness. Outside night has fallen. All is dark inside the church. Jesus is still there but the light that marks his presence is itself a symbol and it fades. This darkness brings great pain. The will is aware of nothing. It has been stripped of all sensible feeling, all intellectual awareness, and all attachments to people, circumstances, and self. But, from time to time, a radiance suffuses it that makes it vividly aware of a presence within the church. When it has learned complete surrender and trust, the will encounters its one beloved who fills the church and the will itself with his wondrous being.

As in the seventh mansions, God suffuses the will with his presence. In a spiritual marriage two become one. Jesus calls us to his heart: we are home at last. And then, miraculously, the dawn comes and light pours through the stained glass windows. Once again figures and patterns are visible. The will stays within the church but serves the world. It relates both to events and individuals. Dwelling in the center of the soul with God, who abides there, the will is joined with the divine will that longs to redeem the world. The contents of the stained glass windows are now loved, not for oneself, but for themselves. Only their good is wished for; only their salvation desired. They are seen in relation to the one divine beloved who longs for the redemption of each.

A second image we may have of the journey of the will lies in the nature of stained glass itself. Each of us is born, perhaps, a particular color of glass. Some of us may be dark in hue; others may be light in hue. We all can be said to represent some color; over our lives we may be a whole series of colors. As the will travels through the mansions, it first becomes very aware of its own coloration. As it moves, it loses more and more of its distinctive color until it becomes one with the light of God. In some ways the color disappears. In other ways it abides, expressing itself in the distinctive characters of people and their creativity. Ah, the wonder of the soul and its range!

This possible nature of souls and their journey is vividly portrayed in a Benedictine Abbey located in Mission, British Columbia. There the stained glass windows are composed of small blocks of glass of most colors found in the rainbow: red, orange, yellow, green, and violet. All the windows spiral upward to a high dome. At the bottom of each window one color appears in multiple numbers, dark, rich, and concentrated. As the window rises, the color becomes more and more faint until, finally at the top, it has become clear glass.

The windows represent symbolically the ascent of the soul to God. Below, near the earth, souls are of many different colors. They exhibit different traits and characteristics, diverse and varied. The closer the soul comes to God, the less of "self" it exhibits. The highest pieces of glass have become clear and translucent: God shines through. As the windows rise and the specific colors become fainter, the pieces of glass become more and more alike. At the top all glass in all windows is the same: each piece lets light fully gleam through. The pieces of glass are of the same color and yet nonetheless retain their individual nature. Each presents light in its own particular way.

Each piece of glass is like a soul. It is a unique thought of God. In the early part of its spiritual journey, it exhibits a definite "self" related to its color and location in any window. As grace works and as the will makes the right choices, the color fades and the soul becomes "transparent." It is transformed into the image of Christ, its will one with the divine will. The Holy Spirit can shine through in creativity. Then the soul in a way can "descend" once again to help and to serve other souls at earlier stages of their journey. The soul has become "another Christ," serving his people. It has achieved "the full stature of Christ" (Ephes. 4:13), reflecting his image fully.

Teresa has described for us the journey of the soul and its transformation into the image of Christ, the perfect reflection of the Father. How precious she has shown the soul of each of us to be: pure crystal or diamond! How difficult and arduous the journey! How manifold the parts of the soul! How splendid the goal, how glorious the final state of the will! In nature every soul is valuable, of inestimable worth. Truly, Teresa teaches, we are in essence precious and lovable.

Notes

1. See the detailed discussions of early Christian authors in B. McGinn, *The Foundations of Mysticism, Origins to the Fifth Century* (New York: Crossroad, 1997), *The Growth of Mysticism, Gregory the Great through the Twelfth Century* (New York; Crossroad, 1996), and *The Flowering of Mysticism, Men and Women in the New Mysticism, 1200–1350* (New York: Crossroad, 1998).

2. Cf. Matt. 22:37 and Mk. 12:30.

3. See especially chapters 14–32, 37–40.

4. Teresa in chapter 4 on the fifth mansions treats in some detail the nature of the devil's activities and how the soul needs to resist them (pp. 354–58).

5. In chapter 3 on the sixth mansions Teresa analyzes different kinds of locutions and how they can be judged genuine as opposed to coming from the imagination or the devil (pp. 374–78). Genuine locutions are not essential to the progress of the will but may occur at this stage of its journey.

6. In chapter 4 on the sixth mansions Teresa gives details of the experience of ecstasy, rapture, or transport (pp. 379–85). All such experiences draw the will inward but should not become the focus of attention or desire.

7. Teresa in chapter 5 on the sixth mansions expands upon the nature of the ecstatic experience of the soul (pp. 386–90). She emphasizes that it is not the work of the devil since it is attended by such great peace. Such experiences, however, are wonderful but not yet the final stage of contemplation.

8. See chapters 7–10 (pp. 397–421).

3
Mother Aloysius of
the Blessed Sacrament:
Training the Soul

*Dwell peacefully in the will
of God, not only his "big"
wills but his "little" wills
of every moment.*

(*Fragrance from Alabaster*, 9)

Teresa has taught us what an inestimable treasure the soul of each person is. At its core abides God. For people to know this and for people to live this truth a long period of spiritual growth is usually required. The goal of the journey that the will undertakes is magnificent but the attainment of the goal can often seem remote. Even to locate the goal can appear as a daunting task. Jesus himself described it as a precious pearl hidden from view.

> The kingdom of heaven is like a merchant in search of fine pearls; on finding one pearl of great value, he went out and sold all that he had and bought it (Matt. 13:45).

Clearly the pearl is the "one thing necessary" that Mary found at the feet of Jesus (Luke 10:42). The "pearl" is also Jesus himself. He is the "image of the invisible God" (Col. 1:15) who can live by grace in our souls. To discover him within is to discover all. He is the "way" (John 14:16) who leads us to God dwelling in our souls. The challenge, however, is to find this pearl. What are the successful methods? What are we human beings to do? What actions does God perform?

In her life as a Carmelite, Mother Aloysius (1880–1961) discovered this precious pearl. She grasped it gently in her hands and generously shared its shining facets with others. These facets are rich and varied. Yet they can all be summed up in one word—Jesus. They all describe his life in the soul. But that life manifests itself in wondrously different ways in different people. Somehow we must recognize it within. Our wills must be molded into a new image to match the will of Jesus.

Mother Aloysius had the gift of discerning the pearl and of helping others to find it also. Her greatest lesson was to teach that the pearl is ever there at every moment and in every situation. It can always be found if we have eyes to see it and the will to search for it. Love for it will draw us on and love will discover it.

In the chapter to follow we will examine this "pearl of great price." We will look at its various facets and wonder at its loveliness. But who was Mother Aloysius, who describes this rare jewel so well? She was a Carmelite who lived first at the Carmel in Boston and then at the Carmel in Concord, New Hampshire. At the time of her death in 1961 she had been a Carmelite for 57 years. During her lifetime she helped many people with her spiritual guidance and her insights into the nature of spiritual growth.

In chapters 1 and 2 we discussed Teresa's detailed description of the journey of the will to God at the center of the soul. She speaks of the stages by which the will comes gradually to be identified with the divine will. Mother Aloysius likewise speaks of growth in holiness. Her focus marvelously complements what we find in Teresa. While Teresa paints a large picture of the will's journey, Mother Aloysius presents us with particular details of this journey. She shows us how God works to draw the will to himself with painstaking care and thoughtfulness.

The writings of Mother Aloysius are still largely unpublished.[1] Some have been collected into a small book called *Fragrance from*

Alabaster, now in its fourth printing. Mother Aloysius shows in particular how God trains the soul in holiness. She teaches in detail what Saint Paul said: "All things work together for good for those who love God, who are called according to his purpose" (Rom. 8:28). In her eyes every soul is lovable, every soul is on a journey to salvation. Each moment God is working out the details of our spiritual development. Each moment is given to us so that we can grow in love.

We shall now examine Mother Aloysius' teachings. In what follows we will frequently let her voice sound because she is as yet so little known.[2]

Events of Our Lives

Mother Aloysius recognizes that every soul is precious and valuable. Each is making a journey to God. This journey, however, is long and arduous. Our souls need to undergo much transformation. What God does is to train us. In this training the present moment becomes very important:

> The little world of each of us with its persons and places, its sunshine and shadows, its joys and its pain, is the one and only Holy of Holies, in which is taber-nacled the will of God, the chosen temple in which alone he accepts our worship. "I shall dwell in their midst" (Deut. 3:12) was his promise, and he is present in every happening. (16)

> The way to the possession of Jesus is in each hourly duty assigned to us. It is the thousand details and actions of daily life. We have only to bring to each of them a spirit of faith, and each moment will hold for us grace, and will hold for us God.

> It is God's desire to manifest himself to us, but he wills to take created forms for this manifesta-tion—forms of persons, events, circumstances, which

call for faith if we are to recognize him, a faith that can discern the divine through and in the human.

For each one of us, the star is shining in the heaven of our souls pointing out to us the place where we shall find Jesus. It is the star of grace contained in the will of God of every moment, that will which leads us to God. (28)

Every event no matter how small, how unimportant, contributes to our spiritual growth. Each molds us so that we can become more like Jesus. Especially valuable are the things that irritate or distress us. How often we want to run away! How often we rebel! How often we cannot believe that this or that horrible event could ever be God at work! But in the most terrible things we are to see the molding and sculpting of our souls by a loving and caring God.

Try to see our Lord working out his plan for your holiness through the vexations and annoyances you meet with. Give yourself sweetly and generously to their purifying action; thus his transforming love can make you his living image; his father will see in you another Jesus seeking only his glory. (5–6)

In using these happenings, we shall find countless opportunities for overcoming our natural self, so given to irritation when things contradict our will, and so ready to think that annoying circumstances justify our showing annoyance. We forget that the occasions do not make us frail but they show what we are.

It is only the light of faith that can enable us to *see through* the various circumstances we meet with and see in them God and his permissive will. To one under the influence of our Lord's spirit instead of her own, these little trials show her our Lord asking for love; and if nature is tempted to complain, the soul that loves is not depressed or discouraged. Rather in this very reaction it sees its weakness, a tendency to watch; and the lover blesses God for the light thus given to know what she must work at, what she must overcome, if she would be pleasing to him. (10–11)

Dwell peacefully in the will of God, not only his "big" wills but his "little" wills of every moment. Look upon each as the footprints of his dear feet in which you are to follow quietly. (9)

Mother Aloysius discerns a purpose in each aspect of our day. God is the author of events. His purpose is to transform us into Jesus. The work is not easy and may involve pain. What we encounter may seem negative and distressful. But Jesus is there.

The pleasure of God, the will of God, is God working to make our souls like himself, and the soul that loves him and co-operates with him in this work of its holiness takes on the ways of the beloved, becoming one with the beloved, for the divine will rules both.

It is that we may take on his ways that Jesus manifests himself in our human nature. He would have us be not only his living image but his very self. (14)

Jesus wishes to continue to the end of time the mystery of the Epiphany by showing himself to us. He offers himself to our adoration and love many times a day, but he always presents himself in a disguise that calls for the exercise of our faith. Jesus comes to us in every annoyance, every trial and suffering we may meet. He comes to us . . . in everything that tends to mortify what is merely natural in us so that the supernatural, the divine, may appear. In all these circumstances he wishes us to pierce the outward appearances by faith and discover *him*. Jesus wishes to show himself *in* each one of us and *by* each one of us. (22)

Suffering

Pain, suffering, distress, or, in short, all that human beings naturally avoid and shun, all that we ever complain of and abhor have a positive purpose. Mother Aloysius asks us to see such things with new eyes. It is not that such sources of suffering are to be thought of as good in themselves. They are not. But they can be seen as God's "disguises." Hidden in them are the means by which we can grow and change. We learn more about ourselves; we learn to say "yes."

> To our faith, the varied happenings of our day are designs of his providence to ask us unawares for a proof of our love—perhaps through a humiliation, an apparent want of appreciation, consideration, or sympathy. He would ask us unexpectedly for an act of patience, of thoughtful charity, a gracious yielding to another. The loving soul will look upon all such occasions with the eyes of faith, never for an instance regarding the exterior circumstances or instrument which have brought them about, but seeing in them only our Lord seeking our love. (30)

All events and happenings are God's instruments. They are to make us grow. They are requests for us to love when we cannot understand and fail to see. They are opportunities to show that we believe and that we are convinced that all things contribute to our growth in holiness.

> Be generous in co-operating with God, whatever the moments hold of things pleasant or painful. It can be an unlooked-for service asked when your day is already planned, an experience when all seems to go wrong. Look upon such an occasion not as a trial, but as an opportunity, and embrace it with all the ardor of a lover who sees at hand a gift for the beloved. I ask this grace for you from our Lady. It will be to share in the grace of her spirit of "handmaid of the Lord"

(Luke 1:38), ready for whatever he wants and whenever he wants it. (35)

> These little trials I called "mere nothings," and so
> they are; yet love for our Lord can transform them into
> something of almost infinite value, and it is for this,
> divine providence permits them to come into our life.
> (45)

The Self Within

What happens as God works and we assent to his will? "Self"
gradually diminishes. We become aware of who we are and how
much we need to grow. Our daily crosses teach us how to learn to
deny the "self" that opposes the formation of Jesus in our souls.
None of these lessons is easy. Rebellion arises in our hearts. But
the royal road of the cross leads to Jesus. He then will mold our
wills so that they reflect the will of God.

> As children of Carmel every one of us is called to
> heroic virtue. Let us not fall short of our vocation. True
> love is wholly forgetful of self and its interests, and its
> happiness consists in spending itself for the beloved.
> (43)

> Self is and always will be with us; consequently we
> cannot expect to be free from selfish impulses and
> tendencies. But love will use them as fuel for the sacri-
> fice. Love will combat them for the sake of the
> beloved, and will be grateful to anyone and grateful
> for anything that will give it an occasion for victory
> over itself. (29)

Mother Aloysius knew well the strength that self could have
in each of us. To discern the valuable and to let the selfish go is a
constant struggle for human beings. She, therefore, calls us to
inner vigilance and to zeal. Our aim is to focus on Jesus.

Must we not admit that often we let ourselves be occupied with thoughts that concern our own interests rather than the great ones of our Lord? Is it not true that these things sometimes occupy us to such an extent as to be the occasion, at least interiorly, of complaints and murmuring which we consider fully justified? What are they in relation to the divine interests? They are mere nothings, and so to forget the great concerns of our Lord and to be intent on one's own selfish aims, is indeed unworthy of a daughter of Teresa. (44–45)

Unselfishness could only be the fruit of the Holy Spirit, the spirit of Jesus, who would have us act as he did—who never pleased himself. (49)

Mother Aloysius makes clear that, when we begin to yield to the Holy Spirit and act less from our own selfish motives, we will experience a cost. The will likes to indulge its own desires but must learn to surrender instead to the divine will. Only by such surrender will it find peace and be able to serve others.

Keep your heart always lifted up and dwell peacefully in the will of your beloved, even his little wills of every moment, for nothing happens but by his permission and for our greater good. Let only one thing have power to move you, the love of God. Try to become more and more penetrated with the thought that God loves you. Believe in that love, and let this thought be to you the source of a joy that nothing on earth can disturb. (7)

Faith alone can discover him to us, and its light is given to show us the treasures we can offer him through the generous acceptance of the divine will.

God's will is our sanctification, but sanctity is whatever God wills that we do, whatever he wills that we be. For each of us he has a life plan worked out to its smallest detailed actions and circumstances, and we shall be holy if our *one* care and preoccupation is to accommodate ourselves and our wills in every detail to this desire of God.

All that our Lord did was to carry out his Father's will. All that we need do is to carry out that same will regardless of the circumstances in which it comes to us—whether it be accompanied with joys or disappointments, gratifications or contradictions, consolations or sacrifices.

Our sole imitation of Jesus is the realization in our lives of the divine will—the complete giving up of ourselves to the will of God as he did, that he may re-express himself in our human nature as other Christs. (12–13)

Like Teresa, Mother Aloysius knew well that the molding of the will into the divine image is a complicated process. It always involves sacrifice. It is also mysterious in nature: often we will not grasp quickly what God is doing. On the one hand, we may be eagerly longing to journey to encounter God in our souls. On the other hand, we may seem to make no progress and to meet only with failure or contradiction. We may too find that we are travelling in darkness such as Teresa described. But in all circumstances our faith must be that God is at work and that all is contributing to our journey to God.

Other People

In particular Mother Aloysius taught that other people in our lives are essential for our progress, however much they seem to hinder and delay our journey. Sometimes, it is true, relationships can prove spiritually harmful and these must be broken or curtailed. But, at other times, we find ourselves with those who must remain part of our lives. With some of these every encounter may seem to be negative and painful. No peace or serenity seems to be possible in such company. It is these very persons, Mother Aloysius suggests, who help us to grow the most. With them our faith is tested, our resolves to love are challenged, and our tolerance and patience are strengthened. God is at work!

> Love and sacrifice are the essentials for a life of union with God. How many opportunities for both lie daily around us. Grace and great graces are hidden in every one, if we are but generous enough to correspond with the designs of divine providence in fashioning them. An ever-increasing faith sees God's designs in even the most trivial things—his design to sanctify us. (17)

> God knows the best human instruments to use in the work of making us saints, which is the work of making us like himself; and they must necessarily be those who will cause us to put aside our own ways and desires and views to take on his. It is a matter of giving up the natural for the supernatural, of following the Holy Spirit instead of our own spirit, of letting that mind be in us that was in Christ Jesus. (3)

Mother Aloysius perceives God's great design for each of us. By all events in our lives the Holy Spirit is forming Jesus in us. Each of us is called on to reflect his nature within. Each of us is unique and our path is entirely individual. There can be, therefore, no single blueprint for spiritual growth, no single road to follow. Instead, God honors our uniqueness by drawing us in individual ways to reflect his Son. It is the Holy Spirit who works this transformation in us. The challenge we face will be to dwell in peace and serenity in the center of our souls. Our wills are to be focused upon God there. Nothing and no one should be able to draw us from God at our center. All things, instead, are to aid both in our journey to that center and to our dwelling there.

To examine frequently our thoughts, words, and actions in the different situations in which we may find ourselves, and to do so in the light that radiates from our Lord, whom we are to imitate—in the light of the Holy Spirit who guided him always—to weigh everything in relation to the divine glory, will show us clearly whether we are under the influence of this Holy Spirit, or our own. (24–25)

Despise the least thought that tends to disturb your peace of soul. Remember you are the tabernacle of the Holy Spirit, and all within the tabernacle is sweetest peace. Cultivate devotion to the spirit of your Emmanuel, and let his love alone have power to move you. Keep your heart always lifted up with ever increasing confidence, and work with holy joy. (21)

Jesus in Our Souls

Mother Aloysius teaches that each soul is a seat of the Holy Trinity. At the center of our souls the Three Divine Persons dwell. We are to remember their presence and direct the attention of our wills to it. This presence is our greatest gift and our wills must come to be absorbed only in it. Circumstances can help or hinder such attention of our wills. Mother Aloysius encourages us to see all externals, whether people or circumstances, as signs of divine grace at work. Inwardly, however, we must do our part. One aspect of our activity will be to cultivate deep, inner silence.

Silence is a necessity for a contemplative soul, and there can be no prayer without it. To each of us is given the obligation to make our cloister and our soul a house of prayer, the home of the Blessed Trinity, a sanctuary of God where we may pass our life listening to him and learning all from him. Let us be watchful over interior silence especially. We are all aware how easily a slight contradiction may call up a multitude of persons and things to occupy our minds. These are "intruders" we are letting into the sanctuary, causing us to lose sight of the divine guest therein and to lose precious time with things that in no way concern his glory. We must bring back our souls to silence and solitude as soon as such thoughts arise to disturb the peace of our interior sanctuary. (51)

It is Jesus in particular whom we will find within. With him we are to hold constant, interior conversation. His interests, his concerns, his glory are to be the focus of our thoughts and will. All other activity of the intellect that centers on unimportant objects or events, simply distracts and delays spiritual growth.

Walk with him always in the way of love and prayer. Strive to shut yourself in the little heaven of your soul, and rest there with him who made you his own. Listen for his voice within and respond to its slightest whisperings. It will urge you to greater fidelity, greater love, and greater generosity for love's sake. (11)

How blessed would we be did we but make the divine heart, the abode of peace and joy, our dwelling place. Then how unworthy of a passing glance even, would we regard the things that too often claim our attention. . . . I beg our Lord to give you a great increase of faith and love. Thus we rise above every disturbance, little or great, and establish ourselves in a region of God's own peace. (12)

Strive to become an interior soul—a soul living unceasing with Jesus and under the influence of his spirit. Seek to dwell with him always, lovingly looking upon him and being filled with his spirit that your life may indeed be "a ray of his life." Thus will you radiate him and shed the sunshine of his grace throughout the world of souls. (29)

Mother Aloysius shows us that the purpose of our interior life with Jesus is to make us share in his work of redemption. Jesus desires to be one with us so that in us he can continue his work of redeeming souls. Only if our will is surrendered to him at the center of our souls can this occur. If our will is abandoned to him and gradually transformed into an image of his will, we shall truly bear fruit. Then we can show that we are the "branches" in Jesus, the "vine" (John 15:5). We shall not be surprised if, in becoming such, we discover that the Father "prunes" us to make us bear "more fruit" (John 15:2).

> I beg Jesus to deepen your awareness of the intimacy with him to which he has called you—even unto union with him. He wants this from us; he needs this from us if we are to win souls for him. This desire of his is hidden in every manifestation of his will—the desire to detach us from ourselves and from all things that we may know that intimacy. (34–5)

> May he reveal to you new depths of love and make his presence felt in your soul as never before—that transforming presence which lightens every burden and makes all crosses sweet for his love's sake. We cannot fathom his ways—all divine. We know only that within our inmost being, surrendered to him and to his will, he is building for eternity. There only will we know in full light his way of love that he would have us walk here unquestioningly in faith. (35–6)

> We dwell not so much where we are as where our heart is—and "where our treasure is, there is our heart also" (Matt. 6:21, Luke 12:34). Our treasure, our divine lover, has ascended to heaven where he tells us himself he has prepared a place for us that where he is, we also may one day be. In the meantime we are to be with him there in spirit and in prayer. This is to "seek the things that are above" (Matt. 6:33). It is to detach

> ourselves from all that is passing to follow him who is
> the way (John 14:6). (43)

Mother Aloysius invites us to abide in the center of our souls
so that we can help to take Jesus to the world. When we become
in close contact with Jesus within our souls, we can then be
witnesses to him in others. We are to radiate Christ to everyone
we meet. In particular, we will come to love others, to work
constantly for their good, and to draw their souls to God. We will
find ourselves resisting self and showing concern for others.

> We can always know, in some degree at least,
> whether or not we are giving our Lord a place of rest
> where all is love for him. The sign is the love we have
> for one another—the willingness we have to sacrifice
> our interests and spend ourselves for others. (20)

> "You shall be witnesses unto me even to the utter-
> most parts of the earth" (Acts 1:8). These words
> addressed to the disciples actually with our Lord, are
> nonetheless addressed to us, for our Lord's mysteries
> are ever present—ever living. To be witnesses unto
> him is to bear testimony to him. It is to give proof of a
> knowledge of him—of his spirit and doctrine. (23)

> Let us withdraw often into the solitude within our
> own interior that we may hear the message our Lord
> may have for us. The commission to be witnesses unto
> him is for all, but the manner of our showing him
> forth is as varied as the souls to whom he speaks. He
> has his personal word for each soul. To one: "Bear ye
> one another's burdens" (Gal. 6:2); to another: "Deny
> thyself and follow me" (Matt. 16:24); "Learn of me
> that I am meek and humble of heart" (Matt. 11:28)
> Whatever that word may be to each of us, it will be a
> call to closer imitation of himself; for only by imitation
> . . . can we hope to make him known. (32)

Heroic Generosity

Mother Aloysius teaches that the will which is absorbed in the Holy Trinity within the soul is the one that proves to be most generous. In our spiritual life we are called to show heroic generosity. This generosity will involve a forgetfulness of self, a reaching-out to others, and a pouring forth of genuine regard, affection, and love to all. None of these is easy. Often they are most difficult. But it is these that will be required.

> The life of nature is always with us, even though our Lord has given us a share in his own life, the life of grace. It is the field of battle where love rejoices to be able to prove its loyalty to the beloved by its generosity.
> This generosity is the visible manifestation of the faith and love of all souls travelling on the way to God, and it always means sacrifice. Unless our giving costs us and is a loving oblation, it is of little value. (3–4)

> Let your heart be full of gratitude to him for his choice of you to give all, and let your joy be that it does cost to give him what he wants. This is real love. (4)

Mother Aloysius had a special gift of understanding how God draws the will to the center of the soul to be transformed by grace. In every passing moment the soul is to learn to deny Jesus nothing. Every moment becomes a request from him; every moment offers a chance to say "yes." Our will is drawn into the will of God. In this holy place we can render to God worship, praise, and love.

We are transformed by love into grateful people, eager to "give all" in return for all the blessings we receive. Every happening and incident speaks to us of God. Each helps to lead our wills to God. Each is suffused with the divine.

Mother Aloysius teaches us that God is the sculptor of our souls. Just as a master craftsman can take a piece of wood or stone and transform it into a wonderful work of art, God changes our souls. Craftsmen often "see" the figure they are about to create already existing in the material on which they work. So the Holy Spirit sees within us the image that the Father has had of us from "before the foundation of the world" (Eph. 1:4). Although we are each unique, this image is nonetheless that of Jesus. The Holy Spirit carefully, quietly, assuredly molds us to the image of Jesus. We will all retain our individual personalities and gifts under this workmanship and yet, through all, the beauty of Jesus will shine.

Sculpted we are. Painful the process may be. Each blow of the artist's instruments wounds. By each stroke we are changed. But the result can be exquisite. As we have all seen in statues of the Virgin Mary, stone and wood can yield works of remarkable beauty. Such statues often teach us much about the spiritual life. Mary usually holds the Christ Child, showing us that we too are to manifest him to others.

In the same abbey mentioned in chapter 2,[3] a magnificent wooden statue of Mary is to be found. Mary, crowned queen of heaven, holds her son, presenting him to the world. If we look closely, we see the intricate and careful work of the artist. From the wood beauty has shone forth. Flaws have been transformed. Potential has been realized. Where before there was only raw material, an image and shape have appeared. Serene peace and loving concern shine from Our Lady's face. Our souls too are wood for the carver. God knows which instruments to use, where to place the wood as it is altered, which workers to summon to the task, and at what rate to have the work done. God transforms us inwardly so that we can pour forth love to our world. Transformed ourselves, we can radiate peace and joy to others.

Mother Aloysius shows us that we are each lovable. We are not perfect but material for improvement and growth. God loves us so much that he transforms us slowly, carefully, and tenderly. We truly become the work of his hands. The "pearl" of great price (Matt. 13:45) is the soul, destined to be transformed into the image of Jesus. This pearl is also, as we suggested at the beginning of this chapter, Jesus, present within the soul, and also the Trinity that abides at its center. Mother Aloysius teaches that we find the pearl in ourselves and for it we sell all and give all. We become inwardly the precious jewel we seek. We are the priceless pearl.

Notes

1. My thanks to Sister Emmanuel of the Carmel in Concord who generously shared with me the unpublished writings of Mother Aloysius.

2. All quotations are from *Fragrance from Alabaster* (Concord, NH: Carmel of Concord, 1961), with minor editorial adjustments. This book was reprinted in December 1999 for the fourth time.

3. Westminster Abbey, located in Mission, British Columbia, Canada.

4
Elizabeth of the Trinity: God within the Soul

*Becoming by an always more
simple, more unitive gaze,
"the splendor of his glory."*

(*Last Retreat,* 162)

In the chapters above we have heard Teresa describe the journey of the will to the center of the soul. We learned from Mother Aloysius how God trains the soul in specific and individual ways so that it grows ever more into the likeness of Jesus. In this chapter we will hear of yet another facet of the spiritual journey. Blessed Elizabeth of the Trinity describes what the will discovers at the center of the soul: the mystery of the indwelling of the Trinity. We find in her writings not only an awareness of the divine presence in the soul but also a deep knowledge of what that presence is like.

In speaking of the presence of God at the center of the soul, we refer to a great mystery. How can God, for whom the whole universe and all human lives are "a drop of dew" or "a grain of sand" (Sir. 18:8), dwell in the soul?

We saw in Teresa that the will travels into the depths of the soul. When the journey is complete, the human will has been transformed, still distinct but now identified with the divine will. At first it may seem that the soul is the large setting with God as the jewel at the center. As the journey proceeds, we soon become aware that it is God, at the center, who entirely suffuses the soul with his being. God's light and presence permeate the soul and enliven it. God draws the will every moment to himself at the center. The more the will surrenders, the more God can fill it and the whole soul. The soul's journey to light is also a filling of the soul by light.

We can say, therefore, that Teresa, describing the soul as an exquisite diamond, teaches us of God's presence at the center of this soul. Elizabeth, for her part, tells us something of what the divine presence in the soul is like. As a special gift, God allowed her to find in an intimate way the Trinity within. In her writings she has revealed details of what the will encounters at the core of the soul.

Elizabeth (1880–1906) was a Carmelite who lived in the Dijon Carmel for the last five years of her brief life.[1] During her long illness she grew closer and closer to God whom she found in a deep and personal way in her soul. There she found the Trinity, whom she often referred to as "my Three."[2] In this chapter we will hear how Elizabeth described the soul and its wondrous divine guest living within. Since her writings, like those of Mother Aloysius, are not greatly known, we will often let her words speak.[3] Again and again she draws aside the veil that conceals the holy and gives us glimpses of heaven existing deep within ourselves. Her writings constantly refer to Scripture, which she studied thoroughly. In passage after passage she found references that helped her to grasp more deeply how God loves the soul and longs to suffuse it with his presence. When God fills the soul, it loves and pours forth this love to others.

Our Soul as a Heaven

Elizabeth teaches that our soul is a paradise. In it God dwells, filling it with "light, love, and life."[4] As she said in one of her letters, "I have found my heaven on earth, since heaven is God, and God is my soul."[5] What we are called to do is to dwell in this heaven at all times. We are to direct our gaze inward and turn our will to focus on the God abiding in our souls.

Remain in me, pray in me, adore in me, love in me, suffer in me, work and act in me. Remain in me so that you may be able to encounter anyone or anything; penetrate further still into these depths. (95)

"Hurry and come down, for I must stay in your house today" (Luke 19:5). The master unceasingly repeats this word to our soul which he once addressed to Zacchaeus. "Hurry and come down." But what is this descent that he demands of us except an entering more deeply into our interior "abyss"?[6] (96)

It is in "this little heaven"[7] that he has made in the center of our soul that we must seek him and above all where we must remain. (108)

"I must stay in your house!" (Luke 19:5). It is my master who expresses this desire! My master who wants to dwell in me with the Father and his Spirit of love, so that, in the words of the beloved disciple, I may have "communion" (1 John 1:3) with them. "You are no longer guests or strangers, but you already belong to the house of God" (Ephes. 2:19), says Saint Paul. This is how I understand "belong to the house of God": it is in living in the bosom of the tranquil Trinity, in my interior abyss, in this "invincible fortress of holy recollection"[8] of which Saint John of the Cross speaks! (61–2)

Like Mother Aloysius, Elizabeth sees God at work at every moment. All events of our lives lead us to this heaven in our souls. There are no moments and no incidents that do not speak of God. All events occur to help the will surrender to God who abundantly loves the soul.

Each incident, each event, each suffering, as well as each joy, is a sacrament which gives God to it; so it no longer makes a distinction between these things; it surmounts them, goes beyond them to rest in its master, above all things. (97)

In order to begin to make this journey to the center where God dwells, Elizabeth teaches us that we must believe in our value and worth. We are lovable and greatly loved.

"We have come to know and to believe in the love God has for us" (1 John 4:16). That is our great act of faith, the way to repay our God love for love; it is "the mystery hidden" (Col. 1:26) in the Father's heart, of which Saint Paul speaks. . . . When it can believe in this "exceeding love" (Ephes. 2:4) which envelops it, we may say of it as was said of Moses, "He was unshakable in faith as if he had seen the Invisible" (Heb. 11:27). It no longer rests in inclinations or feelings; it matters little to the soul whether it feels God or not, whether he sends it joy or suffering: it believes in his love. (101–2)

Once we are convinced that God's will, manifested in every small detail, is for our good, we can learn to accept it willingly, yes, eagerly.

Let us lovingly eat this bread of the will of God. If sometimes his will is more crucifying, we can doubtless say with our adored master: "Father, if it is possible, let this cup pass me by," but we will add immediately: "Yet not as I will, but as you will" (Matt. 26:39); and in strength and serenity, with the divine crucifed, we will also climb our calvary singing in the depths of our hearts and raising a hymn of thanksgiving to the Father. For those who march on this way of sorrows are those "whom he foreknew and predestined to be conformed to the image of his divine Son" (Rom. 8:29), the one crucified by love! (106–7)

Jesus Dwells Within

Everything, Elizabeth affirms, has a purpose and one process is taking place: Jesus is gradually being formed within our souls. Our wills come to be identified with his will. The process is slow but gradually our perspectives change, our desires alter, and our choices become more surely those that Jesus would make.

> I live no longer I, but he lives in me:[9] I no longer want "to live my own life, but to be transformed in Jesus Christ so that my life may be more divine than human,"[10] so that the Father in bending attentively over me can recognize the image[11] of his beloved Son in whom he has placed all his delight.[12] (98)

> "Behold, I stand at the door and knock. If any man listens to my voice and opens the door to me, I will come in to him and sup with him, and he with me" (Rev. 3:20). Blessed the ears of the soul alert enough, recollected enough to hear this voice of the Word of God; blessed also the eyes[13] of this soul which in the light of a deep and living faith can witness the "coming" of the master into his intimate sanctuary. (99)

By becoming quiet within, by serenely accepting God's will, and by surrendering to the Holy Spirit at work in our souls, we are changed. Elizabeth makes clear that our wills must surrender to God's ongoing work.

> Yes, we have become his through baptism, that is what Saint Paul means by these words: "He called them"; yes, called to receive the seal of the Holy Trinity; at the same time we have been made, in the words of Saint Peter, "sharers in the divine nature" (2 Pet. 1:4), we have received "a beginning of his existence" (Heb 3:14) . . . then, he has justified us by his sacraments, by his direct "touches" in our

contemplation "in the depths" of our soul;[14] justified
us also by faith[15] and according to the measure of our
faith in the redemption that Jesus Christ has acquired
for us. And finally, he wants to glorify us, and for that
reason, says Saint Paul, he "has made us worthy to
share in the inheritance of the saints in light" (Col.
1:12), but we will be glorified in the measure in which
we will have been conformed to the image of his
divine Son.[16] So let us contemplate this adored image,
let us remain unceasingly under its radiance so that it
may imprint itself on us; let us go to everything with
the same attitude of soul that our holy master would
have. Then we will realize the great plan by which God
has "resolved in himself to restore all things in Christ"
(Phil. 3:8, 10–14). (105–6)

In her *Last Retreat* in particular Elizabeth speaks of the transformation of the soul in Jesus. The master truly comes to live in
the soul which becomes a heaven in his presence.

"They are transformed from brightness to brightness into his very image by the power of his spirit";[17]
then they are an unceasing praise of glory of the divine
being who contemplates in them his own splendor.
(144)

Then I will be "moved by his spirit" (Rom. 8:14), as
Saint Paul says. I will do only what is divine, only
what is eternal, and, like my unchanging one, I will
live even here below in an eternal present. (155)

What is this "eternal present?" Elizabeth suggests that the
will that is lost in Jesus lives, not its own life any longer, but his
life. When our wills are thus absorbed in Jesus, we cannot fail to
manifest his love and concern for others.

This is Christ's work in every soul of good will and it
is the work that his immense love, his *"exceeding love"*
(Ephes. 2:4), is eager to do in me. He wants to be my

peace so that nothing can distract me or draw me out of "the invincible fortress of holy recollection."[18] It is there that he will give me "access to the Father" and will keep me as still and as peaceful in his presence as if my soul were already in eternity. It is by the blood of his cross that he will make peace in my little heaven, so that it may truly be the repose of the Three. He will fill me with himself; he will bury me with him; he will make me live again with him, by his life: *"Mihi vivere Christus est"*![19] And if I fall at every moment,[20] in a wholly confident faith I will be helped up by him. I know that he will forgive me, that he will cancel out everything with a jealous care, and even more, he will "despoil" me, he will "free"[21] me from all my miseries, from everything that is an obstacle to the divine action. "He will lead away all my powers,"[22] making them his captives, triumphing over them in himself. Then I will have wholly passed into him and can say: "I no longer live. My master lives in me"![23] And I will be *"holy, pure, without reproach"* in the Father's eyes. (156)

Forgetting Self

In order for Jesus to be formed in us and our will to be transformed into his, there must be much denial of self. Elizabeth often speaks of "forgetting self." She urges an unawareness, an oblivion to all the ways our individuality emerges and demands attention. With self very much alive and active, the will cannot be gently drawn to God and altered to match the image of Jesus. We must discern the nature of self and try ever to forget its demands.

> "Abyss calls to abyss" (Ps. 41:8). It is there in the very depths that the divine impact takes place, where

the abyss of our nothingness encounters the abyss of
mercy, the immensity of the all of God. There we will
find the strength to die to ourselves and, losing all
vestige of self, we will be changed into love. (95)

A soul that debates with its self, that is taken up
with its feelings, and pursues useless thoughts[24] and
desires, scatters its forces, for it is not wholly directed
toward God. Its lyre does not vibrate in unison and
when the master plays it, he cannot draw from it
divine harmonies, for it is still too human and discor-
dant. . . . Instead of persevering in praise through
everything in simplicity, it must continually adjust
the strings of its instrument which are all a little out of
tune. (142)

But how do we deal with "self"? Here Elizabeth gives a most
valuable answer. Self is not something to be repressed or
crushed. Instead, it is to be forgotten. Again and again we may
encounter aspects of self in our daily lives. What we are called to
do is consciously and intentionally turn our attention from them.
Simply to forget them. We are not to spend time pondering,
admiring, and valuing those aspects that we consider positive.
We are not to focus endlessly on aspects within that we consider
negative. Instead, we are to keep our eyes on Jesus, trusting in
his guidance and mercy.

To strip off self, to die to self, to lose sight of self. It
seems to me the master meant this when he said: "If
anyone wants to follow me, let him take up his cross
and deny himself."[25] "If you live according to the
flesh," the Apostle [Paul] also says, "you will die, but
if you put to death in the Spirit the works of the flesh,
you will live" (Rom. 8:13). This is the death that God
asks for and of which it is said: "Death has been swal-
lowed up in victory" (1 Cor. 15:54). "O death," says
the Lord, "I will be your death" (Hos. 13:14); that is: O
soul, my adopted daughter, look at me and you will

forget yourself; flow entirely into my being, come die in me that I may live in you! (152)

"Listen, my daughter, lend your ear, forget your people and your father's house, and the King will become enamoured of your beauty" (Ps. 45:10–11).

It seems to me that this call is an invitation to silence: listen . . . lend your ear . . . But to listen we must forget "our father's house," that is, everything that pertains to the natural life, this life to which the Apostle [Paul] refers when he says: "If you live according to the flesh, you will die" (Rom. 8:13). To forget "your people" is more difficult, I think, for this people is everything which is, so to speak, part of us: our feelings, our memories, our impressions, etc., the *self*, in a word! We must forget it, abandon it, and when the soul has made this break, when it is free from all that, the King is enamoured of its beauty. For beauty is unity, at least it is the unity of God! (153–4)

If we strive to "forget" self at all times, what does Elizabeth call on us to "remember"? "Forgetting" is essentially an emptying. It needs to be balanced by a positive focus on "something." Elizabeth makes clear that this "something" is the presence of God within our souls.

And now what does it mean *"to be built up in him"* (Col. 2:7)? The prophet also sings "He has set me high upon a rock, now my head is held high above my enemies who surround me" (Ps. 26:5–6); I think that this can well be taken as a figure of the soul "built up in Jesus Christ." He is that rock on which it is set high above self, the senses and nature, above consolations or sorrows, above all that is not *him* alone. And there in complete self-control, it overcomes self, it goes beyond self and all else as well. (157)

God in our Souls

Elizabeth describes the soul as the exquisite dwelling place of God. Every soul is lovable because it is made in the image of God and God lives within it. Deeper and deeper the will is called to encounter this divine guest abiding in the tabernacle of the soul. The will comes to behold a being of measureless and indescribable beauty. Souls who seek God find

> the furnace of love burning within them which is none other than the Holy Spirit, the same love which in the Trinity is the bond between the Father and his Word. (95)

What does the will encounter when it has traveled to the center of the soul? Elizabeth uses various images to describe the indwelling of the Trinity in the soul. Light, radiance, silence, solitude, holiness—all are aspects of the encounter with the divine.

> The soul that gazes steadfastly on its master with this "single eye which fills the whole body with light"[26] is kept "from the depths of iniquity within it" (Ps. 17:24) of which the prophet complains. The Lord has brought it into "this spacious place" (Ps. 17:20) which is nothing else than himself; there everything is pure, everything is holy! (148)

> The soul that by the depth of its interior gaze contemplates its God through everything in that simplicity which sets it apart from all else is a *radiant* soul: it is "a day that passes on to day the message of his glory." (49)

The soul, Elizabeth says, that chooses silence and solitude will be rewarded by an infusion of divine light. It will be drawn into the vast expanse where God dwells.

> The Divine Being lives in an eternal, immense solitude. He never leaves it, though concerning himself

with the needs of his creatures, for he never leaves
himself; and this solitude is nothing else than his
divinity. . . . The Creator, seeing the beautiful silence
which reigns in his creature, and gazing on her wholly
recollected in her interior solitude, is enamoured of
her beauty and leads her into this immense, infinite
solitude, into this "spacious place" sung of by the
prophet, which is nothing else but himself: "I will
enter into the depths of the power of God" (Ps. 70:16).
Speaking through his prophet, the Lord said: "I will
lead her into solitude and speak to her heart" (Hos.
2:14). The soul has entered into this vast solitude in
which God will make himself heard! (154)

The "single eye" that has come to gaze on God is the will that
now has only one object of its attention. In the deep "abyss"
within the will has found God. There in solitude and stillness it
hears the voice of its beloved. The human and the divine wills,
though ever distinct, have become one.

The soul where God dwells is basically, intrinsically, and
essentially lovable. God, who is love, wants always to love every
soul. God is drawn to the loveliness within each human being.

It is always the desire of the Creator to identify and
to associate his creature with himself! Peter says "that
we have been made sharers in the divine nature" (2
Pet. 1:4); Saint Paul recommends that we hold on to
"this beginning of his existence" (Heb. 3:14) which he
has given us; and the disciple of love tells us: "Now we
are the children of God, and we have not yet seen what
we shall be. We know that when he appears, we shall
be like him, for we shall see him just as he is. And
everyone who has this hope in him makes himself
holy, *just as he himself is holy*" (1 John 3:2–3). To be holy
as God is holy, such is, it seems, the measure of the
children of his love! Did not the master say: "Be
perfect as your heavenly Father is perfect" (Matt.
5:48)? (151)

What God wants most of all is for us, day by day, to become lovelier within. This is possible since the Holy Spirit is ever transforming us into the image of Jesus.

> We can neither give him anything nor satisfy his only desire, which is to exalt the dignity of our soul. Nothing pleases him so much as to see it "grow." (99)

> "Those whom God has foreknown, he has also predestined to become conformed to the image of his divine Son. . . . And those whom he has predestined, he has also called; and those whom he has called he has also justified; and those whom he has justified he has also glorified. What then shall we say after that? If God is for us, who can be against us? . . . Who will separate me from the love of Christ?" (Rom. 8:29–31). This is how the mystery of predestination, the mystery of divine election appeared to the enlightened gaze of the Apostle [Paul]. "Those whom he has foreknown." Are we not of that number? Cannot God say to our soul what he once said through the voice of his prophet: "I passed by you and saw you. I saw that the time had come for you to be loved. I spread my garment over you. I swore to you to protect you, and I made a covenant with you, and you became mine" (Ezek. 16:8). (105)

> He will do everything in you. He will go to the end: for when a soul is loved by him to this extent, in this way, loved by an unchanging and creative love, a free love which transforms as it pleases him, oh, how far this soul will go! (181)

What vision does Elizabeth have of human beings? She emphasizes how beautiful each soul is. She believes that the will is drawn to the center of the soul and, transformed there into the Divine Image, it adores endlessly God who is within. Elizabeth describes what human beings are called to do as they move on their pilgrimage to God at their center:

> Christ said one day to the Samaritan woman that "the Father seeks true adorers in spirit and truth."[27] To give joy to his heart, let us be these true adorers. Let us adore him in "spirit," that is, with our hearts and our thoughts fixed on him, and our mind filled with his knowledge imparted by the light of faith. Let us adore him in "truth," that is, by our works for it is above all by our actions that we show we are true: this is to do always what is pleasing to the Father[28] whose children we are. And finally, let us "adore in spirit and in truth," that is, *through* Jesus Christ and with Jesus Christ, for he alone is the true adorer in spirit and truth. (108)

"Praise of Glory"

Elizabeth was struck in particular by Saint Paul's description of Christians as called to be "praises of the glory" of God's grace (Ephes. 1:11–12). She pondered long on this expression and found in it the essence of the Christian message and the sum total of the Christian calling.

> We have been predestined by the decree of him who works all things according to the counsel of his will, so that we may be *the praise of his glory*.
>
> It is Saint Paul who tells us this, Saint Paul who was instructed by God himself. How do we realize this great dream of the heart of our God, this immutable will for our souls? In a word, how do we correspond to our vocation and become perfect *praises of glory* of the Most Holy Trinity? (111)

Elizabeth pondered long on the phrase "praise of glory," applying it to all human beings. She also realized that we could only become "praises of glory" if we imitated Jesus who perfectly fulfilled this role. She gives a fourfold description of what a praise of glory involves:

> A praise of glory is a soul that lives in God, that loves him with a pure and disinterested love, without seeking itself in the sweetness of this love; that loves him beyond all his gifts and even though it would not have received anything from him, it desires the good of the object thus loved. Now how do we *effectively* desire and will good to God if not in accomplishing his will since this will orders everything for his greater glory? Thus the soul must surrender itself to this will completely, passionately, so as to will nothing else but what God wills.
>
> A praise of glory is a soul of silence that remains like a lyre under the mysterious touch of the Holy Spirit so that he may draw from it divine harmonies; it knows that suffering is a string that produces still more beautiful sounds; so it loves to see this string on its instrument that it may more delightfully move the heart of its God.
>
> A praise of glory is a soul that gazes on God in faith and simplicity; it is a reflector of all the he is; it is like a bottomless abyss into which he can flow and expand; it is also like a crystal through which he can radiate and contemplate all his perfections and his own splendor.[29] A soul which thus permits the Divine Being to satisfy in itself his need to communicate "all that he is and all that he has,"[30] is in reality the praise of glory of all his gifts.
>
> Finally, a praise of glory is one who is always giving thanks. Each of her acts, her movements, her thoughts, her aspirations, at the same time that they

are rooting her more deeply in love, are like an echo of the eternal *sanctus,* [holy]. (112)

Living with Jesus

The "praise of glory" is a soul close to God and especially close to Jesus. It is on Jesus that the will is focused and the eyes are fixed. He is the source of our life. He is our strength, and our hope.

> "Walk in Jesus Christ, rooted in him, built up on him, strengthened in faith and growing in him in thanksgiving" (Col. 2:6–7). Yes, little child of my heart and soul, walk in Jesus Christ: you need this broad road, for you were not made for the narrow paths of here below! Be *rooted* in him. This implies being uprooted from self, or doing everything as if you were, by denying self each time you meet it. *Be built* up on him, high above everything that is passing, there where everything is pure, everything is luminous. (127)

> Be *strengthened in faith*, that is, never act except in the great light of God, never according to impressions or your imagination. Believe that he loves you, that he wants to help you in the struggles you have to undergo. Believe in his love, his *exceeding* love,[31] as Saint Paul says. Nourish your soul on the great thoughts of faith which will reveal to you all its richness and the end for which God has created you! If you live like this, your piety will never be a nervous exaltation as you fear but will be *true*. Truth is so beautiful, the truth of love. "He loved me and gave himself up for me" (Gal. 2:20). That, my little child, is what it means to be true! (128)

Finally, he [Paul] wants me "to grow in Jesus Christ through *thanksgiving*" (Col. 2:6–7): for everything should end in this! "Father, I thank you!" (John 11:41). My master sang this in his soul and he wants to hear the echo of it in mine! But I think that the "new song" (Rev. 14:3) which will most charm and captivate my God is that of a soul stripped and freed from self, one in whom he can reflect all that he is, and do all that he wills. (157–8)

In the first part of her *Prayer to the Holy Trinity* Elizabeth presents her whole picture of who God is and who we Christians are called to be in relation to this wondrous, loving God.

O my God, Trinity whom I adore, help me to forget myself entirely that I may be established in you as still and as peaceful as if my soul were already in eternity. May nothing trouble my peace or make me leave you, O my unchanging one, but may each minute carry me further into the depths of your mystery. Give peace to my soul; make it your heaven, your beloved dwelling and your resting place. May I never leave you there alone but be wholly present, my faith wholly vigilant, wholly adoring, and wholly surrendered to your creative action. (183)

Elizabeth's last words were: "I am going to light, love, and life."[32] In a way these three words sum up her teaching about the beauty and lovable nature of the soul. For her, every moment is one of light. It is filled with God and draws us to God. For her, life is light and is God.

Saint Augustine had said that the human heart was made for God and would never rest except in God.[33] Elizabeth speaks of the soul as the "dwelling," the "heaven," and the "resting place" of God. As such, the soul carries within the God for whom each person longs. But this inner treasure is often hidden. The soul frequently seems to be a vessel filled, not with God, but with self. Thus we must learn to forget self, lose and ignore it so that all our attention can focus on God. Elizabeth suggests that it is our very capacity for light and love that makes each of us very precious and lovable.

Elizabeth points us ever inward. She focuses our gaze on the wondrous nature of the soul. This soul is exquisitely beautiful. Each person should strive to direct the will to this lovely soul within and penetrate deep within it. There it will encounter God who abides in its deepest core. To discover this soul is like coming, during an evening, upon a church lit from within. Blazing out into the night the different colors of the stained glass windows draw us inward. Once within we find, as Elizabeth did, "light, love, and life." The beauty is wondrous; the peace complete. And all this exists within our own souls.

Love for Others

If we make this "journey to the light" and find God dwelling within our souls, what will be the fruit of our encounter? Elizabeth's focus is not only inward. It turns also outward in love for others. By journeying to the center of our souls, we find there total love. What we "see," we become. We are transformed into love:

> This is the measure of the holiness of the children of God: "to be holy as God, to be holy with the holiness of God" (1 John 3:3); and we do this by living close to him in the depths of the bottomless abyss "within." (107)

As we strive in our prayer to encounter this divine love within, we are called to radiate it to others. Thus Elizabeth describes our call as one of total love. One example that she cites is Mary. She describes Mary as one who "adored" God within but who went nonetheless out to others with gracious love and thoughtfulness:

> This did not prevent her from spending herself outwardly when it was a matter of charity; the gospel

tells us that Mary went in haste to the mountains of
Judea to visit her cousin Elizabeth. Never did the ineffable vision she contemplated within herself in any
way diminish her outward charity. (111)

Our whole life, as we think, speak, and act, is to be one of love.
Only Jesus can teach us to behave in this way in all the circumstances of our lives. Yet such love for others is our high calling. If
we love, we are held in God's hands, radiating his light:

> The soul remains under his touch like a lyre, and all
> his gifts to it are like so many strings which vibrate to
> sing, day and night, the praise of his glory! (158)

Elizabeth calls us to be a "praise of glory." In this role we will
abide in the presence of God dwelling in our souls. We will also
radiate his goodness and love to the world in which we live.

Notes

1. The writings of Blessed Elizabeth of the Trinity are being pub-
    lished by the Institute of Carmelite Studies. Thus far two vol-
    umes of *The Complete Works* have appeared.

2. See, for example, her *Prayer to the Trinity*, *Complete Works*, Vol. 1,
    184.

3. We will quote, with minor editorial adjustments, from three of
    her writings, composed in 1906, *Heaven in Faith*, *Last Retreat*, *Let
    Yourself be Loved* and from her *Prayer to the Trinity*, composed in
    1904. All these writings are found in Volume 1 of *The Complete
    Works*. (Volume 2 contains her letters from Carmel.) All Scrip-
    ture references are taken from Volume 1.

4. These were the last words of Elizabeth. See *Light, Love, Life*, ed.
    by C. de Meester (Washington, DC: Institute of Carmelite
    Studies, 1987), 139.

5. *Complete Works*, Vol. 2, *Letter* 122, p. 51.

6. Cf. Ps. 41:8

7. Teresa of Avila, *Way of Perfection*, chap. 28, *Collected Works*, Vol. 2, 142.

8. John of the Cross, *Spiritual Canticle*, Stanza 40:3, *Collected Works*, 629.

9. Cf. Gal. 2:20.

10. John of the Cross, *Spiritual Canticle*, Stanza 12:8, *Collected Works*, 518.

11. Cf. Rom. 8:29.

12. Cf. Matt. 17:5.

13. Cf. Matt. 13:16.

14. John of the Cross, *Spiritual Canticle*, Stanza 19:4-5, *Collected Works*, 520.

15. Cf. Rom. 5:1.

16. Cf. Rom. 8:29.

17. Cf. 2 Cor. 3:18.

18. John of the Cross, *Spiritual Canticle*, Stanza 40:3, *Collected Works*, 629.

19. "For me to live is Christ": Phil. 1:21.

20. Thérèse of Lisieux, poem called "To Live by Love."

21. Cf. Rom. 7:24.

22. Cf. Col. 2:15.

23. Cf. Gal. 2:20.

24. John of the Cross, *Spiritual Canticle*, Stanza 28:7, *Collected Works*, 585.

25. Cf. Matt. 16:24.

26. Cf. Matt. 6:22.

27. Cf. John 4:23.

28. Cf. John 8:29.

29. John of the Cross, *Spiritual Canticle*, Stanza 3:77, *Collected Works*, 705.

30. John of the Cross, *Spiritual Canticle*, Stanza 3:1, *Collected Works*, 673.

31. Cf. Ephes. 2:4.

32. See above, note 5.

33. *Conf.* 10.27.37.

Conclusion: Hidden Pearls

*The truth is that the
treasure lies within
our very selves.*

(*Interior Castle*, V.1.2)

Jesus compares the kingdom of heaven to a "precious pearl" for which one sells everything (Matt. 13:45–46). What we have suggested in this book is that the soul with its divine guest at its core can be thought to be this "pearl." We have suggested also that it is essential for all people to be aware that this "pearl" is within and makes every person lovable. These women of Carmel have taught us much about this soul. They have offered us "hidden pearls" of wisdom to help us understand our spiritual journey. These three, beholding the world that we all see, looked deep within and saw concealed treasures. Teresa discerned much about the soul. Mother Aloysius grasped the meaning of everyday events and circumstances for our spiritual growth. Elizabeth came to understand features of the divine indwelling. All three emphasize the need for us to radiate love to others.

Teresa describes the nature of the soul, comparing it to a crystal or diamond castle. She says that this castle has seven levels or "mansions" through which the will travels. In the last or "seventh" mansions God dwells. As the will journeys, it is transformed. Gradually the human and divine will come to be identified. The journey is a long and complicated one. The castle is there in everyone but not all people make this journey. Some people stay outside the castle; some travel some distance within; some go right to the center to encounter God. For everyone the whole journey is possible. Teresa calls all of us to make this journey.

Mother Aloysius likewise speaks of the beauty of the soul. She discerns with penetrating vision how God slowly trains and teaches this soul. She sees that all events and circumstances are arranged by an all-loving God for the growth and development of each person's spiritual life. All things are to be seen in the light of the loving action of God. Negative situations, pain, and suffering somehow are part of the divine plan for our good. During our lives certain circumstances help to deliver the "self." This self we must come to know fully. This self we must learn to deny. Other circumstances show us all the virtues we need to cultivate. Yet other circumstances lead us to enter deep within and draw us on our journey to encounter God in our souls.

Elizabeth tells us much of the "hidden pearl" that is our soul. She encountered in a deep and penetrating way the presence of the Trinity in her soul. She knows that the soul can be the heaven of God and that we are invited not merely to go there but to dwell there moment by moment.

Elizabeth teaches that the self can hinder the journey of the will to God within. She describes what this self is and shows how its activities can be recognized and resisted. With self forgotten, God becomes all. This God acts as the source of all creativity. The will, yielded to the divine will, adores and creates the beautiful for others.

These three women of Carmel describe different aspects of the beauty of the soul. How precious, how wonderful each human being, made in the image of God, is! How essentially lovable we all are, whatever we may think of ourselves or others may think of us! Whatever our actions, whatever our wounds, God dwells within summoning us to journey ever deeper into his presence. We are all called to encounter Jesus, the light of the world, ever perfectly reflecting the Father.

The following poem sums up the wonder of each human being as God's special creation. God delights in us to such an extent that he makes "his home in us" (John 14:23). With astonishment we learn who we are and to what we have been called.

God's Gifts

You have given me
eyes to see your beauty,
ears to hear your praise,
touch to feel your presence,
a nose to sense your fragrance,
a tongue to taste your sweetness,
and a mouth to sing your glory.

You have given me
imagination to dream of your splendors,
memory to recall your deeds,
a mind to trace your workings,
and desire to long for you.

You have given me
hands to render you service,
legs to kneel in prayer,
feet to run after you,
and arms to embrace you.

You have given me
silence to seek you,
solitude to find you,
a heart to beat for you,
and a will to surrender
in peace
to your infinite love.

Biographies

*How true it is that once
we have caught sight of the
Divine Beauty and heard his voice,
all other loveliness pales before it.*

(Mother Aloysius, *Fragrance from Alabaster*, 1)

Life of Saint Teresa of Avila

Chronology

March 28, 1515	Teresa de Cepeda y Ahumada born in Avila
1535	Teresa enters the Monastery of the Incarnation of Avila
1537	Teresa professes her vows
August, 1562	Teresa founds the "reformed" convent of St. Joseph's
1565	*Book of her Life*
1566–1567	*Way of Perfection*
1569	*Soliloquies*
1567–1582	Seventeen foundations of new convents of the Reform
1574	*Meditations on the Song of Songs* (2nd version)
1577	*Interior Castle*
October 4, 1582	Teresa dies at convent in Alba de Tormes at sixty-seven years of age
1622	Teresa is canonized a saint

1970   Teresa is declared a doctor of the Church
                            by Pope Paul VI

Principal Works

Life; Meditations on the Song of Songs; Way of Perfection; Soliloquies;
Interior Castle; Letters; Foundations

Life of Mother Aloysius
of the Blessed Sacrament

Chronology

February 18, 1880   Alice Rogers born in Billerica (near
                     Boston) to Timothy and Mary Rowe Rogers
1901–1903   Aloysius taught school
September 12, 1904   Aloysius enters Boston Carmel
January 20, 1905   Aloysius receives habit as Sister Aloysius of
                     the Blessed Sacrament
February 2, 1906   Aloysius professes her vows
1918–1936   Aloysius is frequently prioress of Boston
                     Carmel
1945   Aloysius founds Carmel in Concord, New
                     Hampshire
May, 1955   Aloysius' golden jubilee
April 16, 1961   Aloysius dies at eighty-one years of age

Collection of Writings

Fragrance from Alabaster

Life of Blessed Elizabeth of the Trinity

Chronology

July 18, 1880	Elizabeth Catez born in military camp of Avor to Joseph and Marie Catez
July 22, 1880	Elizabeth's baptism
February 24, 1883	Elizabeth's sister, Marguerite Catez, is born
October 2, 1887	Elizabeth's father, Joseph Catez, dies
October, 1888	Elizabeth begins playing piano; becomes accomplished pianist
April 19, 1891	Elizabeth's First Communion
June 8, 1891	Elizabeth's Confirmation
1893	Elizabeth wins first prize at piano
August 2, 1901	Elizabeth enters Carmel
December 8, 1901	Elizabeth takes habit of Carmel (clothing)
January 11, 1903	Elizabeth professes her vows
November 9, 1906	Elizabeth dies at twenty-six years of age

Principal works

Heaven in Faith (1906); *Last Retreat* (1906); *Let Yourself be Loved (1906); Prayer to the Trinity* (1904); *Letters from Carmel (1901-1906)*

Selected Bibliography

Let nothing disturb you;
Let nothing dismay you;
All things pass.
God never changes.
Patience attains
All that it strives for.
Those who have God
Find they lack nothing.
God alone suffices.

(Teresa of Avila's Bookmark)

Elizabeth of the Trinity

Translations

The Complete Works of Elizabeth of the Trinity. Translated by A. Kane. Washington, DC: ICS Publications, 1984. Volume 1.

The Complete Works of Elizabeth of the Trinity. Translated by A. E. Nash. Washington, DC: ICS Publications, 1995. Volume 2.

Secondary Sources

Balthasar, H. Urs von. *Two Sisters in the Spirit: Thérèse of Lisieux and Elizabeth of the Trinity.* San Francisco: Ignatius Press, 1992.

Benedictines of Stanbrook Abbey. *Reminiscences of Sister Elizabeth of the Trinity.* Westminster, MD: Newman Press, 1952.

Benedictines of Stanbrook Abbey. *The Praise of Glory.* London: G. Chapman, 1962.

Borriello, L. *The Spiritual Doctrine of Blessed Elizabeth of the Trinity, Apostolic Contemplative,* trans. J. Aumann. New York: Alba House, 1986.

De Meester, C. OCD, *Elizabeth of the Trinity, Light, Love, Life,* trans. A.
    Kane, OCD. Washington, DC: ICS Publications, 1987.
Philipon, M.M., OP. *Sister Elizabeth of the Trinity: Spiritual Writings.*
    London: G. Chapman, 1962.
_____. *The Spiritual Doctrine of Sister Elizabeth of the Trinity.*
    Westminster, MD: Newman Press, 1947.

Mother Aloysius of Carmel

Cooney, A.J., OCD. "Give All—and Ever" in *Portraits in American Sanctity.*
    Ed. J.N. Tylenda, SJ. Chicago: Franciscan Herald, 1982, Chapter 25.
Discalced Carmelites of Concord. *Mother Aloysius of Carmel, Fragrance from
    Alabaster.* Concord, NH: Carmel of Concord, 1961.

Teresa of Avila

Translations

The Collected Works of St. Teresa of Avila. Translated by K. Kavanaugh, OCD
    and O. Rodriguez, OCD. 2nd ed. Washington, DC: ICS Publications,
    1987. 3 volumes.
The Complete Works of St. Teresa of Avila. Translated by E. A. Peers. London:
    Sheed and Ward, 1946. 3 volumes.
The Letters of Saint Teresa of Jesus. Translated by E. A. Peers. Westminster,
    MD: Newman Press, 1950.

Secondary Sources

Bielecki, J. *Teresa of Avila: Mystical Writings.* New York: Crossroad, 1994.
Boersig, T. M., "Teresian Spirituality." *Contemplative Review* 15 (1982),
    37–42.
Burrows, R. *Fire Upon the Earth: Interior Castle Explored.* Denville, NJ:
    Dimension, 1981.
Capalbo, B. *Praying with St. Teresa.* Translated by P. Clifford, Grand
    Rapids, MI: Eerdmans, 1997.
Chorpenning, J. F. *The Divine Romance: Teresa of Avila's Narrative Theology.*
    Chicago: Loyola Univ. Press, 1992.
_____. "The Literary and Theological Method of the *Interior Castle,*"
    Journal of Hispanic Philology 3 (1979), 121–33.

Clissold, S. *St. Teresa of Avila.* London: Sheldon Press, 1979.

Dicken, E. W. T. *The Crucible of Love: A Study of the Mysticism of St. Teresa of Jesus and St. John of the Cross.* New York: Sheed and Ward, 1963.

Dubay, T. *Fire Within: St. Teresa of Avila, St. John of the Cross and Gospel on Prayer.* San Francisco: Ignatius Press, 1989.

du Boulay, S. *Teresa of Avila: Her Story.* Ann Arbor: Hodder and Stroughton, 1991.

Egan, H. D., SJ. "St. Teresa of Avila (1515–1582)" in *Christian Mysticism: The Future of a Tradition.* Edited by H.D. Egan, SJ. New York: Pueblo, 1984, 118–64.

Egan, K. J. "The Significance for Theology of the Doctor of the Church: Teresa of Avila" in *The Pedagogy of God's Image: Essays on Symbol and the Religious Imagination.* Edited by R. Masson. Chico, CA: College Theological Society, 1981, 153–71.

Frolich, M. *The Intersubjectivity of the Mystic: A Study of Teresa of Avila's "Interior Castle."* Atlanta, GA: Scholars Press, 1993.

Galilea, S. *The Future of Our Past: The Spanish Mystics Speak to Contemporary Spirituality.* Notre Dame, IN: Ave Maria Press, 1985.

Green, D. *Gold in the Crucible: Teresa of Avila and the Western Tradition.* Longmead, Shaftesbury, Dorset: Element Books, 1989.

Gross, F.L. *The Making of a Mystic: Seasons in the Life of St. Teresa of Avila.* Albany, NY: SUNY Press, 1993.

Hamilton, E. *The Great Teresa.* London: Burns and Oates, 1963.

————. *Saint Teresa, A Journey in Spain.* New York: Charles Scribner's Sons, 1959.

————. *Servants of Love: The Spirituality of Teresa of Avila.* London: Darton, Longman and Todd, 1975.

Hatzfeld, H. *Santa Teresa of Avila.* New York: Twayne, 1969.

Hellwig, M. "St. Teresa's Inspiration for Our Times." *Carmelite Studies* 3 (1982), 212–24.

Howe, E. T. *Mystical Imagery: Santa Teresa de Jesús and San Juan de la Cruz.* New York: P. Lang, 1988.

Humphreys, C. *From Ash to Fire: An Odyssey in Prayer: A Contemporary Journey through the Interior Castle of Teresa of Avila.* New Rochelle: New City Press, 1992.

Lincoln, V. *Teresa, A Woman: A Biography of Teresa of Avila.* Albany, NY: SUNY Press, 1984.

Luti, J.M. *Teresa of Avila's Way.* Collegeville, MN : Liturgical Press, 1991. *The Way of Christian Mystics* 13.

Marie-Eugene, F. *I am a Daughter of the Church.* Notre Dame, IN: Fides, 1955.

————. *I Want to See God.* Notre Dame, IN: Fides, 1953.

Medwick, C. *Teresa of Avila: The Progress of a Soul.* New York: Knopf, 1999.

Peers, E. A. *Handbook of the Life and Times of St. Teresa and St. John of the Cross*. London: Burns and Oates, 1954.

_____. *Mother of Carmel: A Portrait of St. Teresa of Jesus*. London: SCM Press, 1946.

_____. *Saint Teresa and Other Essays*. London: Faber and Faber, 1953.

_____. *Studies of the Spanish Mystics*. London: S.P.C.K., 1960. 3 volumes.

Rahner, K. trans. E. Quinn. "Teresa of Avila: Doctor of the Church" in *Opportunities for Faith*. New York: Seabury, 1970, 123–26.

Sackville-West, V. *The Eagle and the Dove*. London: M. Joseph, 1943.

Seelaus, V. "The Feminine in Prayer in the Interior Castle," *Mystics Quarterly* 21 (1987), 201–14.

Slade, C. *St. Teresa: Author of a Heroic Life*. Berkeley: Univ. of Calif. Press, 1995.

Sullivan, J., ed., *Centenary of St. Teresa*. Washington, DC: ICS Publications, 1984. *Carmelite Studies* IV.

Sullivan, S.M. "The Castle of Teresa of Avila: The Inward and Outward Journey," *Magistra* 7 (2001), 85-95.

Swietlicki, C. "The Problematic iconography of Teresa of Avila's Interior Castle," *Studia Mystica* 11 (1988), 37–47.

Thomas, F. and Gabriel, F., eds. *St. Teresa of Avila: Studies in her Life, Doctrine and Times*. London: Burns and Oates, 1963.

Williams, R. *Teresa of Avila*. Harrisburg, PA: Morehouse, 1991.

Acknowledgments

I wish to express my gratitude to the Institute of Carmelite Studies in Washington, DC, for material quoted from their editions of Teresa of Avila and Elizabeth of the Trinity. I thank also the Carmel of Concord, NH for material quoted from *Fragrance from Alabaster*.

I wish to thank the Basilian Fathers at St. Mark's College, University of British Columbia, for encouraging my study of Christian spirituality, especially that of Teresa of Avila. I thank also Sr. Emmanuel of the Carmel of Concord who generously shared the unpublished writings of Mother Aloysius with me. To Arden Williams who entered the manuscript onto the computer with diligent care I express my gratitude. I also thank Gary Brandl and all at New City Press who gave such careful attention to my manuscript.

LIVING THE LITTLE WAY OF LOVE
With Therese of Lisieux

By John Nelson

"This little book is full of charm and insight on the 'Little Way.' It explains St. Therese's spirituality in an uncomplicated way, and Nelson offers his insights to help anyone who wishes to take this 'way' to a better spiritual life.... Each chapter of the book takes up one of Therese's principles and expands upon it with clear and simply-written exposition.... The book is recommended to all who wish to expand their own spirituality and to those who wish to know more about Therese of Lisieux."

Catholic Library World

"Wonderfully grasping St. Therese's 'little way,' John Nelson shows profoundly yet simply how holiness is possible for everyone. Through other classic spiritual texts, he provides for Therese a perceptive, beautiful setting."

Kieran Kavanaugh, O.C.D.
Carmelite author and translator

ISBN 1-56548-133-X, paper, 5 3/8 x 8 1/2, 192 pp.

THERESE OF LISIEUX
A Discovery of Love, Selected Spiritual Writings
By Terence Carey, O.C.D. (ed.)

Once thought of as merely a saint of miracles and devotion, more recent studies of Therese's writings have uncovered an entirely new dimension. It is this "new" aspect of Therese that this selection of her writings would like to examine. Carey shows that beyond her humility and apparent littleness there is a powerful message of holiness to be discovered. Her teaching is both fresh and enchanting and is centered on the fundamental essence of God: love. "My way is all confidence and love," she writes, "I don't understand souls who fear a friend so tender."

Carey begins his work with a concise but informative biography, followed by a short explanation of Therese's writings, inviting you to read ahead and discover her way. This book is for you if you are looking to familiarize yourself more with Therese of Lisieux, or if you have already embarked on a spiritual journey and would like guidance along the way.

"The selections from the *Story of a Soul* and the *General Correspondence* of Therese seek to show her to be an authentic teacher of the spiritual life."

Theology Digest

"Dividing her life into five periods, Carey illustrates her attractive personality through her own writings."

Prairie Messenger

ISBN 1-56548-072-4, paper, 5 3/8 x 8 1/2, 144 pp.

To Order Phone 1-800-462-5980
www.newcitypress.com